FAITH NOTES

[Jesus said,] "Everyone then who hears these words of Mine and does them will be like a wise man who built his house on the rock."
(Matthew 7:24)

A CHRIST-CENTERED **SURVIVAL KIT** FOR YOUNG MEN

Michael W. Newman

CONCORDIA PUBLISHING HOUSE · SAINT LOUIS

DEDICATION

To Layne and Wyatt.
"These are written so that you may believe that Jesus is the Christ, the Son of God, and that by believing you may have life in His name" (John 20:31).

Published by Concordia Publishing House
3558 S. Jefferson Ave., St. Louis, MO 63118-3968
1-800-325-3040 • cph.org

Manufactured in USA.

2 3 4 5 6 7 8 9 10 11 34 33 32 31 30 29 28 27 26 25

MY NAME IS:

....

PRINT YOUR NAME HERE

I AM THANKFUL TO WALK IN FAITH WITH JESUS, MY SAVIOR!

....

SIGN YOUR NAME HERE

QUICK-START GUIDE

These short and quick-to-read devotions may be exactly what you need most right now. **You are living in one of the most challenging seasons of life.** How do you get through it? Not by letting the world's agenda and attitude fill your notebook of life, but by taking note of the good, wise, and exciting life Jesus has given you. Along the way, your Savior will bless you with the survival tools you need most.

How can you use this devotional? Here are some tips:

- ☐ Read one sentence. That's right. Each devotion opens with a one-sentence, bite-sized, faith-growing nugget to chew on. Even if you don't like to read, you can look at one sentence every day.
- ☐ If you take another day to read the "God's Word Speaks" and "Need a Little More?" sections included with each devotion, you'll have two or three days worth of daily devotional material for each topic.
- ☐ Use the "Faith Notes" section of each devotion to journal, think, pray, doodle, and apply what you've read.
- ☐ Find subjects that match your needs in the "Contents" pages or the "Index of Subjects" (p. 217) and let God's Word provide help and guidance when and where you need it most.

- ☐ Finally, don't worry about reading the book from front to back. Choose the topic that fits your situations and interests in the moment.

Jesus is the true friend you need. He is stronger than your struggles. He teaches you and leads you faithfully. He carries you through every joy and sorrow, every challenge and blessing. Jesus loves you and cares about you. His death and resurrection for you prove it. He will never abandon you.

Trust Him on your faith journey.

CONTENTS

THE ANXIETY SURVIVAL KIT

THE MISTAKE SURVIVAL KIT

THE FAMILY AND HOME SURVIVAL KIT

THE CHARACTER SURVIVAL KIT

THE PURITY SURVIVAL KIT

THE RELATIONSHIP SURVIVAL KIT

THE BODY SURVIVAL KIT

THE VIRTUAL LIFE SURVIVAL KIT

THE THOUGHTS AND FEELINGS SURVIVAL KIT

THE SPIRITUAL LIFE SURVIVAL KIT

THE FRIEND SURVIVAL KIT

THE FUTURE SURVIVAL KIT

1 BIG WORRY: YOUR IDENTITY

ONE-SENTENCE DEVOTION

Listen carefully, young man of God: your identity—the core and foundation of who you really are—is this: you are a loved and treasured child of God, who gives everything for you on your challenging journey of life; believe it and don't let anyone tell you otherwise.

GOD'S WORD SPEAKS

And [Jesus] opened His mouth and taught [His disciples]. (MATTHEW 5:2)

NEED A LITTLE MORE?

Jesus cares so much about you that He takes time to talk to you. He teaches you through His Word. He shares His wisdom. And He gives you His strength and peace. He calls you His friend and brother through Baptism. Don't ever let anyone convince you that you are anything else but God's beloved child. Jesus proved His love for you when He gave His life for you on the cross. Be careful, because other people, the world, the devil—even your own heart and mind—will pile on worry, comparison, stress, fear, shame, anger, hopelessness, and negativity. Resist that noise. Jesus overcame it all—even death—to make you His beloved son. Know who you really are because of Jesus, your Savior.

FAITH NOTES

Note how life makes you feel about yourself—
both the bad and the good.

Circle what you need to pay more attention to.

2

BIG WORRY: FEELING ANXIOUS

ONE-SENTENCE DEVOTION

Worry and anxiety will try to dominate your brain, but you receive rest and relief in Jesus, who provides peace and strength even when life is grinding you down.

GOD'S WORD SPEAKS

[Jesus said,] "Blessed are the poor in spirit, for theirs is the kingdom of heaven." (MATTHEW 5:3)

NEED A LITTLE MORE?

Jesus said that you are blessed even when worry starts to gnaw on your soul and spirit. How could He say such a thing? Because He is with you and working for you even when life stinks. Feeling worried is no match for the work of God's grace. These feelings won't defeat you; they only highlight the protecting and peace-giving presence of Jesus. Remember, worry doesn't rule you. Your Baptism made you a citizen of God's kingdom. God is the one who rules in your life. His rule will give you peace (see

John 14:27). Substitute worry with prayer. That's right. Pray every time worry tries to crush you (see Matthew 6:34; Philippians 4:6–7). Watch how God's peace will restore your soul.

FAITH NOTES

It's time to give your anxiety to God! Write down what's worrying you and stressing you out. Then face the day with Jesus' peace.

3

BIG WORRY: HOW YOU LOOK

ONE-SENTENCE DEVOTION

Look in the mirror and mentally embrace your uniqueness—your face, your hair, your height, your build—because God created you as an irreplaceable and beloved blessing to the world.

GOD'S WORD SPEAKS

[Jesus said,] "But even the hairs of your head are all numbered. Fear not, therefore; you are of more value than many sparrows." (MATTHEW 10:30–31)

NEED A LITTLE MORE?

Jesus said, "Even the hairs of your head are all numbered." That's not an excuse for skipping a few haircuts or letting bedhead be your choice of hairstyle. But it's true that your hair—its color, texture, volume, waves, cowlicks—is no accident. You may wish you could change it and may even make temporary alterations, but your Creator gave it to you as a gift to help make you uniquely you! That's true about all of your physical features. God created you to be you and to make your unique mark on the world. Don't let an ideal version of what you THINK you're SUPPOSED TO look like lead you to despise WHO YOU REALLY ARE. You are a one-of-a-kind creation who is so loved that Jesus Himself paid the ultimate price for your sins so you can one day go to heaven. Comparing yourself to the latest social media portrayals of the perfect dude will only discourage you. You are a gift to the world—and to the people in your life. There's only one you—and God loves and delights in you.

FAITH NOTES

Write down a physical feature of yours that bothers you most. THEN PUT A BIG **X** OVER IT.

....

....

....

....

....

....

....

....

....

....

Ask someone you trust to tell you what he or she likes about your looks. Write those down and cherish the blessing of being uniquely you.

4

BIG WORRY: WORLD EVENTS

ONE-SENTENCE DEVOTION

The world is broken (messed up ever since Adam and Eve sinned in the Garden of Eden), but Jesus is the Savior of the world who hears your prayers and walks with you through every anxious thought you have about suffering, stress, and tragedy.

GOD'S WORD SPEAKS

[Jesus said,] "In the world you will have tribulation. But take heart; I have overcome the world." (JOHN 16:33)

NEED A LITTLE MORE?

If you focus on all the bad news in the world, you're going to feel really terrible and anxious. Every day, there are enough terrible, awful, depressing, and tragic events to grind you down into an anxiety-crippled, hopeless mess of a human being. Bad things happen. Tragedies will strike even your friends and family. This world groans in sin and decay. You live in a very stressful time. But that's why God sent His Good News and His

Word of life—Jesus. Jesus came to save you and to be a counterbalance to the craziness. In order to cope with world events, you need a steady dose of God's helpful and life-giving Word. Read the Bible. Take time every day for devotion and prayer. Listen to the encouragement of the Gospel at home and in church. Don't let the onslaught of the twenty-four-hour news cycle fool you. Life is not all bad news. Jesus is with you and has overcome the bad events of the world.

FAITH NOTES

List sources of bad news in the left column and sources of the Good News in the right column. Stop paying attention to so many of the bad news sources and focus on the Good News sources to create balance and peace in your life.

5

BIG WORRY: PARENTS INTERFERING

ONE-SENTENCE DEVOTION

If you feel like your parents are embarrassing you, try this secret strategy that's rooted in the way God gives you His grace and love: thank them, tell them you love them, and then watch the awkwardness fade away.

GOD'S WORD SPEAKS

And [Jesus] went down with [His parents] and came to Nazareth and was submissive to them. And His mother treasured up all these things in her heart. And Jesus increased in wisdom and in stature and in favor with God and man. (LUKE 2:51–52)

NEED A LITTLE MORE?

(Honest moment: some of you reading this WISH you had a parent who cares or YEARN to have a parent who is involved in your life.) Know that God, your heavenly Father, loves you and is with you. That's a reality check if you groan every time your mom or dad talks to your teacher, your coach, your principal, your friends, or their friends. If you can't handle any more parental interference, you can do two things: be grateful and communicate. If your parents are involved in your life, it's a sure sign they love you. You can thank them for all the blessings they provide and the love they give you. You can also talk to them politely about what might make you feel less awkward. Even Jesus asked His mom and dad, "Why were you looking for Me? Did you not know that I must be in My Father's house?" (Luke 2:49). Jesus communicated His heavenly Father's plan of salvation through the young man standing before them. Then He was obedient to and honored His earthly parents. Exercising your gratitude and communication muscles will help you be a faithful son and will calm your anxiety when your parents get involved in your life.

FAITH NOTES

Take time to sit with your parents so you can tell them you love them and appreciate all they do. (They may pass out, so be ready, but they'll really appreciate this.) If you don't have a parent to talk to, share this with a grandparent or the person who shows you care and love in your life. Note below how it felt to you and what responses you received.

....

....

....

....

....

6

BIG WORRY: SCHOOLWORK

ONE-SENTENCE DEVOTION

You're not going to school to become a perfect person with perfect grades; instead, you're there to try your best and work hard, try new experiences, see what you're good at, and share your God-given gifts with others as you live under Jesus' forgiveness and grace.

GOD'S WORD SPEAKS

[Jesus said,] "And he who had received the five talents came forward, bringing five talents more, saying, 'Master, you delivered to me five talents; here, I have made five talents more.' His master said to him, 'Well done, good and faithful servant. You have been faithful over a little; I will set you over much. Enter into the joy of your master.'" (MATTHEW 25:20–21)

NEED A LITTLE MORE?

The pressure is high to get straight A's in school and to be the best in everything. You may feel it. You may even be able to make those grades (and possibly be filled with anxiety in the process). But achieving perfection or being the best isn't what school is about. School isn't in your life so you can prove yourself worthy of love from your parents or the world. School doesn't exist to label you as a success or a failure. In school, you can try out lots of stuff—reading, writing, math, sports, music, art, science, technology—and discover the talents God has given you. School helps you find out what you like to do and what you're good at. As you discover your unique gifts, you can travel the adventure of seeing how those gifts will bless the world. God created you, loves you, and gives you His grace through the sacrifice of Jesus on your behalf. Walk patiently with God as you grow and discover more about the life He designed for you. Take a little pressure off yourself as you enjoy the journey of discovering what you like best.

FAITH NOTES

List your favorite and least favorite subjects and activities in school. Think about what job or vocation your interests and talents might steer you toward.

7

BIG WORRY: FRIENDS

ONE-SENTENCE DEVOTION

Life can sometimes cause you to feel friendless and criticized by people around you, but remember that Jesus is the friend who is always with you, always loves you, and always has a great purpose for exactly who you are.

GOD'S WORD SPEAKS

[Jesus said,] "Behold, I am with you always, to the end of the age." (MATTHEW 28:20)

NEED A LITTLE MORE?

Sometimes being in groups of people can cause a lot of anxiety. You can feel pressure to conform to other people's expectations, or you may feel judged about the way you look and act. You may feel self-conscious about your appearance, about your clothes, or about your ability to fit in. But you're part of a crowd for a reason. People need you. Your uniqueness contributes to the world. God created you to bring His blessing and presence to others through your extraordinary individuality. No one can replace you. Your job isn't to blend in but to boost the quality of the crowd with all God is doing through you. Because Jesus gave you new life when He overcame sin and death and then rose from the grave, you have something to add wherever you go. And don't be afraid. If you're a quiet presence in the group or if you're a boisterous addition, Jesus is walking with you to strengthen you, help you, and use you to bless others according to God's plan for you and them.

FAITH NOTES

Google **extrovert** and **introvert**. Note which word fits you best and how your personality adds to the groups you're in.

8

BIG WORRY: PEER PRESSURE

ONE-SENTENCE DEVOTION

Why let liars and losers steer you in the wrong direction when Jesus, who cares about you so much that He died to give you eternal life, guides you where you really need to go in this life?

GOD'S WORD SPEAKS

And Jesus answered them, "See that no one leads you astray." (MATTHEW 24:4)

NEED A LITTLE MORE?

Maybe you've heard the old saying that misery loves company. People who are crashing and burning always want you to crash and burn with them. Why would you go along with that? You don't need messed-up people to like you, and you don't need to please people who pressure or threaten you. Jesus made it clear that a lot of fakes will appear in your life (see Matthew 24:24). Don't believe them. Don't fall for the pressure to drink alcohol while under age, use drugs, bully, lie, have sex outside of marriage, use pornography, or give in to other destructive temptations they toss your way. Trust your Savior and the godly and truthful people He places in your life. They will keep you out of the crowd that is headed to disaster and on the good road that leads to a fulfilling life in Christ.

FAITH NOTES

What trustworthy person has Jesus placed in your life? Thank that person for being there for you. Go to him or her for advice when you're feeling peer pressure.

Write a Bible verse below that helps you when you feel peer pressure.

1

BIG MISTAKE: PERFECTIONISM

ONE-SENTENCE DEVOTION:

Admit it: you know that you're imperfect and flawed, which is why you need what God gives freely every day: His gifts of forgiveness, grace, and strength.

GOD'S WORD SPEAKS

And great crowds followed Him from Galilee and the Decapolis, and from Jerusalem and Judea, and from beyond the Jordan. (MATTHEW 4:25)

NEED A LITTLE MORE?

Babies can't do much at all. If they're not cared for, fed, nurtured, and loved, they won't survive. Guess what? You were a baby once, and you're still weak and helpless in so many ways. That's why you shouldn't get so frustrated or depressed when you struggle to learn something—like math, reading, making your bed, driving, or shooting free throws. You don't know everything, and you can't do everything automatically. You make mistakes. Some things will always be hard.

The people who followed Jesus were the same way. They were a bunch of unholy, mistake-prone human beings from many places and backgrounds (the Decapolis had a reputation for being very unholy). But Jesus welcomed them anyway. He taught them and helped them. Jesus welcomes you too. He is patient with you, He loves you, and He helps you. Jesus gave His life for you to forgive your mistakes and to let you face tomorrow with His new beginning.

FAITH NOTES

List a few things that are easy for you and a few things that are hard. Think of how you can help other people who struggle with what you think is easy. Then think about who you can ask for help with the things that are difficult for you.

EASY	DIFFICULT

2

BIG MISTAKE: ALWAYS HAPPY?

ONE-SENTENCE DEVOTION

Sometimes you are bummed out, sad, or in a bad mood; when you feel those emotions, Jesus is always present as your source of comfort and help.

GOD'S WORD SPEAKS

[Jesus said,] "Blessed are those who mourn, for they shall be comforted." (MATTHEW 5:4)

NEED A LITTLE MORE?

No one is happy all the time. Sometimes you feel angry, disappointed, or sad. You may feel a certain emotion because you failed. You may feel a certain emotion because someone hurt you or a situation didn't work out the way you hoped it would. Feeling those feelings is not wrong. If you're bummed out about something, you need to process it and walk through it. But you also need to know your source of help and restoration—your Savior, who overcame all that is bad and disappointing in this world. Jesus came into the world to carry your burdens and to comfort you when you feel distressed. That's why people who mourn can be blessed: Jesus brings blessings to bummed-out minds and hearts. When Jesus says, "In the world you will have tribulation. But take heart; I have overcome the world" (John 16:33), He means it!

FAITH NOTES

One important answer to emotions that get you down is God's Word. It is an authentic resource for lasting strength and joy. Here's the beginning of a Bible-reading plan to get you into God's Word:

- ☐ Start with one of the Gospels (Matthew, Mark, Luke, or John). You'll learn about Jesus' life.
- ☐ Then read Galatians through Colossians. These are short letters to Christians, with great teachings for faith and daily life.
- ☐ Next, go back to Acts, the story of how Christianity began and how God works in your life.

3

BIG MISTAKE: UNKINDNESS TO YOURSELF

ONE-SENTENCE DEVOTION:

You don't need to be so hard on yourself; God is FOR you, not against you.

GOD'S WORD SPEAKS:

[Jesus said,] "For God so loved the world, that He gave His only Son, that whoever believes in Him should not perish but have eternal life. For God did not send His Son into the world to condemn the world, but in order that the world might be saved through Him." (JOHN 3:16–17)

NEED A LITTLE MORE?

Did you know that Jesus is called the "kindness of God" (Titus 3:4)? God is kind to you. As sinners, we don't deserve such caring treatment. But God doesn't exist to be mean to you, to make you feel guilty, or to zap you because you did something wrong. God loves you. He is for you. And He sent Jesus to save you. If God's kindness meant sending His own Son to do away with your mistakes by dying on the cross and rising from the dead, why shouldn't you show yourself some kindness? Don't beat up and criticize yourself. You are God's precious child! Go easy on yourself as a receiver of God's grace. Jesus said, "I came not to call the righteous, but sinners" (Mark 2:17). That means Jesus didn't come to see if you can be perfect; in His perfection, He came to make sure you're forgiven.

FAITH NOTES:

How are you being too hard on yourself? Write how God feels about that based on John 3:16–17.

4

BIG MISTAKE: SEXUAL IMPURITY

ONE-SENTENCE DEVOTION

Let's be honest: living a sexually pure life isn't easy, but walking in the pathway of purity will fill you with peace so you can serve God's will and bless others—and if you fail or fall, be assured that Jesus will forgive you and give you a fresh start.

GOD'S WORD SPEAKS

[Jesus said,] "Come to Me, all who labor and are heavy laden, and I will give you rest. Take My yoke upon you, and learn from Me, for I am gentle and lowly in heart, and you will find rest for your souls. For My yoke is easy, and My burden is light." (MATTHEW 11:28–30)

NEED A LITTLE MORE?

Part of being a man is having sexual desires. That desire isn't meant to torture you; it exists so you can, one day, bless your wife with your focused affection and so you can become skilled at self-control—something you will need every day as a man. Yet sexual desire can also pull you into habits that will hurt you and your relationships. Fueling lustful thoughts with pornography, habitual masturbation with impure videos, seeing how far you can get with girls, and having sex before marriage can fill you with guilt and can harm your ability to be healthy in relationships. But you're not alone in this challenge. Living by faith means that Jesus steps up to carry the burden of your temptations and failures, giving you strength and grace to live in sexual purity. Jesus invites you to approach Him humbly and prayerfully so He can carry your burdens. Jesus walks with you so you can experience His help, forgiveness, and strength to be a pure and self-controlled man of God.

FAITH NOTES

In 2 Corinthians 5:17, Christ says you are a new creation. What new-creation actions will you commit to for the purpose of sexual purity? Note them below.

5

BIG MISTAKE: GRUDGES

ONE-SENTENCE DEVOTION

Holding things against people will crush you under the weight of hatred and resentment, but letting go of your grudges and letting God deal with them frees you to live in God's forgiving joy.

GOD'S WORD SPEAKS

[Jesus said,] "It is finished," and He bowed His head and gave up His spirit. (JOHN 19:30)

NEED A LITTLE MORE?

Jesus told a story about laborers in a vineyard who received the same pay even though some worked a full day and some put in only one hour. The workers who sweated out the whole day resented this move—even though they had already agreed to the amount of pay they would receive. The master said to the angry workers, "Am I not allowed to do what I choose with what belongs to me? Or do you begrudge my generosity?" (Matthew 20:15). Grudges cause you to miss out on being thankful for God's goodness. Resenting people robs you of joy and gets you stuck in unthankfulness. When Jesus said, "It is finished," He released you from every possible grudge God had against you. That means you can release any grudge you might have against someone else. You don't live in bitterness toward others anymore; you live in the beautiful gift of forgiveness.

FAITH NOTES

Gratitude can help cure grudges. Write a list of ten things you're most thankful for below.

....

....

....

....

....

....

....

....

....

....

6

BIG MISTAKE: SHAME

ONE-SENTENCE DEVOTION

Shame makes you think that you are unworthy and should go into hiding, but Jesus rejected shame on the cross and rose from the dead to give you His worthiness and to set you free from shame.

GOD'S WORD SPEAKS

Then [the master of the wedding banquet] said to his servants, "The wedding feast is ready, but those invited were not worthy. Go therefore to the main roads and invite to the wedding feast as many as you find." And those servants went out into the roads and gathered all whom they found, both bad and good. So the wedding hall was filled with guests. (MATTHEW 22:8–10)

NEED A LITTLE MORE?

Jesus' parable of the wedding feast makes it very clear that God's invitation to join Him matters more than your unworthiness to be at His party (or in His presence). This is really important to understand and to trust. You will do all kinds of things that will make you ashamed. That's what sinful people do—even when they don't mean to. Shame will try to cover you with a heavy, dark cloak of unworthiness and disgrace. Shame will try to convince you that you don't belong. Shame will tell you that you are bad. But shame is telling only half-truths. If you were on your own, shame might be right, but you are not alone. Jesus' death and resurrection pulled away the heavy shroud of shame and brought the light of God's grace into your life. Because Jesus carried your shame, God sees you as His perfect and shiny new creation. No hiding is needed. You're at the party as an honored guest. Jesus made sure of it. Now you serve Him and live for Him with your head held high.

FAITH NOTES

Tell God what makes you want to hide. Ask Him to carry your shame and let you live in His grace.

7

BIG MISTAKE: DENYING YOUR FAITH

ONE-SENTENCE DEVOTION

God loves you so much that He calls you to return to Him no matter how far you've strayed.

GOD'S WORD SPEAKS

Now Peter was sitting outside in the courtyard. And a servant girl came up to him and said, "You also were with Jesus the Galilean." But he denied it before them all, saying, "I do not know what you mean." (MATTHEW 26:69–70)

NEED A LITTLE MORE?

Do you go to church? Do you pray? Do you read the Bible? Do you have meaningful Christian friendships? Or have you strayed from God? Peter, one of Jesus' disciples, denied that he knew Jesus. He did it three times. But instead of Jesus saying, "Three strikes and you're out," Jesus restored Peter. Jesus sought Peter and brought him back (see John 21:15–19). You need to know that even if you deny your faith, stop going to church, and stray from your Christian life, Jesus will always seek you and welcome you back to Himself. Jesus forgives you, restores you, and lets you enjoy His amazing gift of life with Him.

FAITH NOTES

Today may be the day Jesus calls you back to Himself. How is He showing His love for you again today?

8

BIG MISTAKE: SELF-HARM

ONE-SENTENCE DEVOTION

Get help, give God another day to come through, and trust His grace and love for you when you feel the darkness of depression, pain, and hopelessness—but don't harm yourself; don't do it.

GOD'S WORD SPEAKS

Then when Judas, His betrayer, saw that Jesus was condemned, he changed his mind and brought back the thirty pieces of silver to the chief priests and the elders, saying, "I have sinned by betraying innocent blood." They said, "What is that to us? See to it yourself." And throwing down the pieces of silver into the temple, he departed, and he went and hanged himself. (MATTHEW 27:3–5)

NEED A LITTLE MORE?

Judas didn't need to end his life. True, he made a huge mistake by betraying Jesus, and he regretted what he had done, but he missed one important point: Jesus takes the biggest mistakes, the greatest sins, the worst impossibilities, and the most hopeless situations and turns them around. He forgives, He restores, He helps, and He saves. Even when you think that no possible solution to your problem exists, Jesus can work a miracle. Watch for it. Wait for it. Ask for it. Get help. Your Savior gave His life for you so your life would never have to be lost to the hurt of this broken world. Trust Him today.

FAITH NOTES

If you're hurting and feeling hopeless, pray a prayer asking God to help you right now. If you have thoughts about harming yourself, call or text 988 (the National Suicide and Crisis Lifeline in the United States and Canada). Or reach out to a parent, pastor, or friend before you take any action.

1

FAMILY HINT: RIVALRY

ONE-SENTENCE DEVOTION

Each person in your family is unique and fully loved by God, so keep this in mind when you're tempted to compare yourself to them and be assured that your heavenly Father compares you to no one.

GOD'S WORD SPEAKS

But the angel said to him, "Do not be afraid, Zechariah, for your prayer has been heard, and your wife Elizabeth will bear you a son, and you shall call his name John." (LUKE 1:13)

NEED A LITTLE MORE?

This might seem like a strange statement in some situations, but you are not in competition with your family members. Not everything is even or fair all the time, but that doesn't mean you're being left behind or ignored. Everyone has his time to shine, to experience things, and to be celebrated. In the Bible, Elizabeth thought she was hopelessly forgotten, and she was terribly criticized by her family and friends because she couldn't have children. But at the right time, according to His plan for the world, God came through for her. Joseph was treated badly by his brothers and even sold into slavery, but in God's timing, things turned around for him too. In His perfect plan and timing, God sent His Son to live, teach, heal, serve, suffer, die, and rise again—for you. God sees you and knows your situation. He hasn't forgotten you. Your time will come. As you wait for your uniqueness to shine, celebrate with your brothers, sisters, parents, cousins, and other family members, knowing that God will lift you up in His timing for you.

FAITH NOTES

Instead of being at odds with your parents or siblings, compliment each one today.

2

FAMILY HINT: TRUST THE PROGRAM

ONE-SENTENCE DEVOTION

Your parents' rules may really bug you, and you may feel like ignoring them, but go with the program for a while, trusting that, through your parents, God is shaping your life with His love and protection and that He will open doors to more independence at the right time.

GOD'S WORD SPEAKS

Jesus answered [John the Baptist], "Let it be so now, for thus it is fitting for us to fulfill all righteousness." Then he consented. And when Jesus was baptized, immediately He went up from the water, and behold, the heavens were opened to Him, and He saw the Spirit of God descending like a dove and coming to rest on Him; and behold, a voice from heaven said, "This is My beloved Son, with whom I am well pleased." (MATTHEW 3:15–17)

NEED A LITTLE MORE?

Curfews, chores, and rules about cleaning your room and doing homework can feel annoying. As you grow up, you want to be more independent, and the restrictions you have at home may seem unnecessary. But if you obey your parents cheerfully and go with the program, greater trust and responsibility will come your way. You will have a stronger relationship with them and more freedom as you get older. When John the Baptist was growing up, he learned about the Messiah from his father, Zechariah. Still, he hesitated when Jesus came to him to be baptized. However, John's knowledge of who Jesus was caused him to obey Jesus, who in turn pleased His heavenly Father with His own obedience. John followed God's plan, and his faith gave him the courage to point others to the Savior. Trust God's plan and program at home as you submit to your parents. God's love and blessing will carry you through.

FAITH NOTES

What rules at home do you need to follow better? Make one improvement today.

3

FAMILY HINT: YOUR BIG FAMILY

ONE-SENTENCE DEVOTION

When your family isn't functioning well, or maybe isn't even around, you are still embraced by your big eternal family: God as your heavenly Father and fellow Christians who are brothers and sisters in faith.

GOD'S WORD SPEAKS

Now when all the people were baptized, and when Jesus also had been baptized and was praying, the heavens were opened, and the Holy Spirit descended on Him in bodily form, like a dove; and a voice came from heaven, "You are My beloved Son; with You I am well pleased." (LUKE 3:21–22)

NEED A LITTLE MORE?

You've got a big family beyond your immediate family. God makes you His precious child in Baptism. The words He spoke at Jesus' Baptism apply to you because your Baptism clothed you with Jesus' life, death, and resurrection (see Galatians 3:27; Romans 6:3–4). God gathers His baptized children into the big family called the church. The church is much more than a building; it is the gathering of God's forgiven children who love one another and share Jesus' love with everyone in need. The church provides you with brothers and sisters in faith who love you, pray for you, and walk with you through joys and challenges. Take heart: if your immediate family is broken or gone, you're still a beloved member of the big family of God.

FAITH NOTES

If you don't have a church, look for one you can attend. If you are part of a church, thank someone there for something he or she has done to reassure you that you are part of the church family.

4

FAMILY HINT: GIVING IN

ONE-SENTENCE DEVOTION

Jesus gave up everything to save you, and He gives you all you need—that's why you don't have to get your way all the time; sometimes giving in is your greatest strength.

GOD'S WORD SPEAKS

[Jesus said,] "Blessed are the meek, for they shall inherit the earth." (MATTHEW 5:5)

NEED A LITTLE MORE?

Meekness doesn't mean you're wimpy, and kindness is not a weakness. Meekness is an attitude that means you are close to God—just like Moses: "Now the man Moses was very meek, more than all people who were on the face of the earth" (Numbers 12:3). Moses spoke with God face to face, just like a friend (see Exodus 33:11). Jesus, the Suffering Servant of God, is called the "kindness of God" (Titus 3:4). Both Moses and Jesus practiced self-sacrifice for God and His people. Their attitude was that life was not all about them; it was about rescuing God's beloved children. The meekness and kindness God gives you will bless your family, bring them joy, and share God's love. Don't think you always have to argue or oppose your family. Walk in God's gifts of meekness and kindness. Serve. Listen. Help out. Give in. Watch how you will "inherit the earth."

FAITH NOTES

Try not to get your way for a whole week. Write down what you notice when you give in.

5

FAMILY HINT: SAY YOU'RE SORRY

ONE-SENTENCE DEVOTION

Jesus' humility changes your heart so you can know that saying "I'm sorry" gets you much farther than arguing.

GOD'S WORD SPEAKS

[Jesus said,] "As you go with your accuser before the magistrate, make an effort to settle with him on the way, lest he drag you to the judge, and the judge hand you over to the officer, and the officer put you in prison." (LUKE 12:58)

NEED A LITTLE MORE?

Jesus didn't come to argue with us. He didn't come to make Himself look good or to prove that we were worthless sinners. Just the opposite. He humbled Himself and died in our place on the cross so we could be saved, forgiven, and made right in God's eyes. When you feel like justifying yourself, proving your point, and arguing, pause to see the Savior, who blessed you with His humble sacrifice. Humbling yourself, listening, and saying "I'm sorry" will help your situation more than you can imagine. Even if you feel like you haven't done anything wrong, saying "I'm sorry" (and meaning it) shows that you care about the other person's feelings and needs. You will never go wrong in your family by showing Jesus' self-sacrificial love.

FAITH NOTES

Next time an argument or conflict happens at home, try not to defend yourself. Instead, listen humbly, don't interrupt, and say, "I'm sorry."

6

FAMILY HINT: COMMUNICATION

ONE-SENTENCE DEVOTION

God values your voice, and He put you in this world to share your thoughts and feelings so the people in your life—starting with your family—will be blessed by Jesus' unique work in you and through you.

GOD'S WORD SPEAKS

Then one of [the healed leprous men], when he saw that he was healed, turned back, praising God with a loud voice; and he fell on his face at Jesus' feet, giving Him thanks. Now he was a Samaritan. Then Jesus answered, "Were not ten cleansed? Where are the nine? Was no one found to return and give praise to God except this foreigner?" And He said to him, "Rise and go your way; your faith has made you well." (LUKE 17:15–19)

NEED A LITTLE MORE?

The healed man in Luke 17 returned to Jesus and said, "Thank You." He communicated his gratitude to Jesus. And because of it, he received the added blessing of Jesus' word of sending and salvation. Communication works wonders. You may feel like ignoring people in your family, grunting at your parents when they ask you questions, or groaning because you Just. Don't. Want. To. Talk. But caring communication is worth practicing. Words build relationships and let you practice showing God's love and gratitude to people in your life. Jesus is called God's "Word" who became "flesh" (John 1:14) for a reason. Communication from God brought you into His grace and eternal life. Your communication with family will show you care and will build them up in love.

FAITH NOTES

Two assignments:

1. Start a conversation with your parents at dinner or at the end of the day by telling them three things you enjoyed about the day. Jot your ideas below.

....

....

....

....

2. Next time your mom or dad ask you a question, try to look them in the eyes and give a kind answer of at least two sentences. Write those sentences below.

....

....

....

....

7

FAMILY HINT: WHEN IN DOUBT, SHOW LOVE

ONE-SENTENCE DEVOTION

When you're under pressure and feel like getting angry or lashing out in frustration, do the opposite—just as God did for you—and follow His path of speaking and acting with love.

GOD'S WORD SPEAKS

When Jesus saw His mother and the disciple whom He loved standing nearby, He said to His mother, "Woman, behold, your son!" Then He said to the disciple, "Behold, your mother!" And from that hour the disciple took her to his own home. (JOHN 19:26–27)

NEED A LITTLE MORE?

It's easy to speak and act in loving ways when you feel good and everyone is being nice. But when the pressure is on, when you disagree with someone, when someone is bugging you, or when you are tired, hangry, or stressed, you may feel like letting some mean comments and gestures fly. But Jesus gives you a new life and a different path. His guidance for you means that when pressure is ramped up, you have the resource of His love and grace to meet the challenge. As Jesus hung on the cross in great pain, rejected by God, carrying our sin, He asked John the disciple to take care of His mother. New life in Jesus lets kindness overtake adversity and meanness every time. When the pressure is on, see how God's love shines in you and through you.

FAITH NOTES

Draw what love looks like to you below.

8

FAMILY HINT: YOU'RE HERE TO SERVE

ONE-SENTENCE DEVOTION

So much of God's love, blessing, and affirmation has been poured into your life that these things can overflow freely from you into the lives of your family with heaps of service, help, and self-sacrificial love.

GOD'S WORD SPEAKS

Jesus, knowing that the Father had given all things into His hands, and that He had come from God and was going back to God, rose from supper. He laid aside His outer garments, and taking a towel, tied it around His waist. Then He poured water into a basin and began to wash the disciples' feet and to wipe them with the towel that was wrapped around Him. (JOHN 13:3–5)

NEED A LITTLE MORE?

During your childhood, you got used to receiving a lot. You were fed, clothed, and driven to places; your tears were dried, skinned knees were bandaged, and clothes were washed. Because of everything you received, you began to think that everyone existed to serve you and to let you have your way. But you're not in a family just to be a consumer. You're there to contribute, to help, and to give—just as God has done for you. Jesus put this servant heart into you. As He faced His crucifixion, He prayed, "My Father, if it be possible, let this cup pass from Me; nevertheless, not as I will, but as You will" (Matthew 26:39). He put His own desires aside to give His life for you on the cross. Just before His crucifixion, Jesus washed His disciples' feet. He said to them, "For I have given you an example, that you also should do just as I have done to you" (John 13:15). Jesus is the one who washes away our sin and gives us new life. Now, whether it's making your bed, cleaning your room, helping with the yard or around the house, sharing video game time with your family members, or just being kind, your life of faith serves and contributes to your family and to the world.

FAITH NOTES

What needs to be done around the house that you can help with right now? Make a list below. Then go for it.

1
WHAT IT MEANS TO BE A MAN: ADMIT YOU'RE WRONG

ONE-SENTENCE DEVOTION

Being a man doesn't mean you imitate the proud, trash-talking, aggressive, or confrontational ways of the world but that God's humility and servanthood overtake your heart and shape everything you say and do.

GOD'S WORD SPEAKS

From that time Jesus began to preach, saying, "Repent, for the kingdom of heaven is at hand." (MATTHEW 4:17)

NEED A LITTLE MORE?

Why was repentance the main subject of Jesus' preaching? Because we all need it. We all have a pride problem. Have you noticed how you fall into the trap of being smug, superior, and self-important? You don't want to admit you're wrong. You want to defend and justify yourself—even when you are caught in an act of disobedience or complete error. Repentance turns you around. It brings you back to God and away from a destructive path. That's what Jesus did for you. He turned you back from getting lost in arrogant sin by letting your sin destroy Him. Jesus humbled Himself to death for you. He is more man than any of us—a real man. In Luke 18, Jesus told a parable about a self-righteous Pharisee and a lowly and sinful tax collector. The Pharisee boasted about how good he was. But Jesus said, "The tax collector, standing far off, would not even lift up his eyes to heaven, but beat his breast, saying, 'God, be merciful to me, a sinner!' I tell you, this man went down to his house justified, rather than the other. For everyone who exalts himself will be humbled, but the one who humbles himself will be exalted" (vv. 13–14). That's how God shapes a real man. You're a real man when you humbly admit you're wrong and ask for forgiveness.

FAITH NOTES

See how you can replace the phrase "But I (insert excuse here)" with "I'm sorry. I was wrong" this week.

2

WHAT IT MEANS TO BE A MAN: MAKE GOD'S WORD YOUR LIFELINE

ONE-SENTENCE DEVOTION

Let's be real: everything in this world will fade away and decay except the life-giving Word of God—a real man's ultimate resource.

GOD'S WORD SPEAKS

[Jesus] answered [the devil], "It is written, 'Man shall not live by bread alone, but by every word that comes from the mouth of God.' " (MATTHEW 4:4)

NEED A LITTLE MORE?

When Jesus was being tempted by the devil in the wilderness, the devil tried to lead Jesus to trust in temporary things, like bread that only satisfies for a while. You face the same temptation. The devil, the world, and your own sinful flesh will try to lure you into placing all your passion and energy into temporary pursuits. What are you tempted to pour your life and attention into? Girls? Money? Cars? Your physique? Popularity? Partying? Academics? Beware! All of it will turn to dust one day.

But God's Word endures forever (see Isaiah 40:8). The life He gives by grace through His Son will never fail. His wisdom, strength, and peace are a firm foundation for you. Reading, hearing, and knowing God's Word will shape you into a man who makes a difference and shines the light of God's hope and truth to the world.

FAITH NOTES

How are you doing with your Bible-reading plan? Here's part 2 of a plan to get you into God's Word:

- ☐ Read Genesis, the first book of the Bible. It includes key teachings about life and God's work.
- ☐ Then read Romans to see how to apply Jesus' words to your everyday life.
- ☐ Then read the Psalms. They are prayers and songs that will reflect your experience and help you grow in your walk with God.
- ☐ Next, tackle Isaiah to see the amazing promises and encouragement of God.
- ☐ After that, keep going with books of the Bible of your choice. Be ready for an adventure and for blessing!

3

WHAT IT MEANS TO BE A MAN: STAND UP FOR THE WEAK

ONE-SENTENCE DEVOTION

A life of faith in Jesus doesn't mean joining the crude chorus of bullies and brutes in the world; it means defending the weak just as Jesus rescued you in your weakness with His love and grace.

GOD'S WORD SPEAKS

[Jesus said,] "Blessed are those who hunger and thirst for righteousness, for they shall be satisfied." (MATTHEW 5:6)

NEED A LITTLE MORE?

The fact that there are so many mean, trash-talking, bullying, egotistical, insecure, arrogant, and violent men in the world shows that the price of entry into that kind of life is cheap. It is a wide and easy road to travel with no thought, no effort, no bravery, and no faith required. Becoming a bad sport, a social media troll, an intimidator of others, and a hot-tempered and ill-mannered cad takes no effort at all. Just go with the flow of sinful and fallen flesh. But Jesus carved out a narrow road that defends the weak, serves the least of these, and shines His right and good ways to all. The price of admission to this way of life was absorbing the brutal consequences of sin and spilling His blood for you. Jesus became weak, gave His life, and rose victoriously from death to place you on the life-giving path that the world can't imagine or manufacture. Your grace-given hunger and thirst for righteousness will bless the world with what really satisfies as you stand up for the weak by sharing Jesus, who said, "I am the bread of life; whoever comes to Me shall not hunger, and whoever believes in Me shall never thirst" (John 6:35).

FAITH NOTES

Write some words below that describe how you may have been slipping into being mean and unrighteous. Then put an **X** through each word and replace it with a word that describes the new life Jesus gives.

4

WHAT IT MEANS TO BE A MAN: SELF-CONTROL

ONE-SENTENCE DEVOTION

As you see how God resisted lashing out at us fallen sinners who push Him away, you will also see the Holy Spirit's fruit of self-control in front of you, demonstrating quiet strength and showing love even when you are provoked.

GOD'S WORD SPEAKS

[Jesus said,] "But I say to you, Do not resist the one who is evil. But if anyone slaps you on the right cheek, turn to him the other also." (MATTHEW 5:39)

NEED A LITTLE MORE?

Almost every day, you will be tempted to enter a vortex of anxiety, anger, and meaningless arguments. People will drag you into their mess. Social media will entice you to add snarky comments. Antagonists will try to pull you into their divisive chorus. Bullies will provoke you into physical fights. But Jesus gives you a life that is secure in Him and in the power of His love.

He endured the worst kind of treatment and took all the world's meanest sins on His shoulders, suffering and dying for even these. Because Jesus did this, your life isn't in the vortex of controversy. Resistance to violent words and actions will accomplish more than being confrontational. Restraint with a peaceful attitude will make more progress than forceful fighting. "A soft answer turns away wrath" (Proverbs 15:1). God will take care of the irksome irritator. His Word directs you, "Beloved, never avenge yourselves, but leave it to the wrath of God, for it is written, 'Vengeance is Mine, I will repay, says the Lord'" (Romans 12:19). Practice self-control as you depend on God's justice and Word to bring calm strength to troubled times.

FAITH NOTES

What gets your temper going? Write what could help you calm down and some people who can intervene if a bully is badgering you.

....

....

....

....

....

....

....

....

....

5

WHAT IT MEANS TO BE A MAN: ACTIVE IN PRAYER

ONE-SENTENCE DEVOTION

Jesus is strong, but He isn't the silent type, and He shapes you in the same way: as an active, vocal communicator with Him in prayer.

GOD'S WORD SPEAKS

[Jesus said,] "Ask, and it will be given to you; seek, and you will find; knock, and it will be opened to you. For everyone who asks receives, and the one who seeks finds, and to the one who knocks it will be opened. Or which one of you, if his son asks him for bread, will give him a stone? Or if he asks for a fish, will give him a serpent? If you then, who are evil, know how to give good gifts to your children, how much more will your Father who is in heaven give good things to those who ask Him!" (MATTHEW 7:7–11)

NEED A LITTLE MORE?

Through Jesus, your faithful advocate and defender, God gives you the gift of prayer. When you cry out to Him, praying in Jesus' name, He hears you and responds.

God promised in Psalm 50:15, "Call upon Me in the day of trouble; I will deliver you, and you shall glorify Me." Prayer is for your benefit and blessing. The Bible says, "Do not be anxious about anything, but in everything by prayer and supplication with thanksgiving let your requests be made known to God. And the peace of God, which surpasses all understanding, will guard your hearts and your minds in Christ Jesus" (Philippians 4:6–7). Even if you can't put together words that capture your anguish, the Holy Spirit brings your speechless groans to God (see Romans 8:26). God loves you so much that He wants to hear from you. He invites you to ask, seek, and knock as a man of prayer.

FAITH NOTES

Your prayers can be shaped by the acronym ACTS: Adoration (praising God), Confession, Thanksgiving, and Supplication (making requests). Use these parts of prayer as you talk to God today.

6

WHAT IT MEANS TO BE A MAN: SHOW LOVE

ONE-SENTENCE DEVOTION

Your strength as a man is strongest when it reflects the greatest strength ever shown in the history of the world: God loving the world so much that He gave His only Son to sacrifice His life for fallen and broken humanity.

GOD'S WORD SPEAKS

[Jesus said,] "A new commandment I give to you, that you love one another: just as I have loved you, you also are to love one another. By this all people will know that you are My disciples, if you have love for one another." (JOHN 13:34–35)

NEED A LITTLE MORE?

Your greatest strength as a man is not shown in how much you can bench press. It is not revealed in how loud or forceful you can be. It is not demonstrated in your ability to impress girls, what clothes you wear, the fragrance you choose, or how skilled you are in sports or in the classroom. Your greatest strength as a man is in shown in how you share the love God has shown and shared with you through Jesus. God's Word guides you: "Do nothing from selfish ambition or conceit, but in humility count others more significant than yourselves. Let each of you look not only to his own interests, but also to the interests of others. Have this mind among yourselves, which is yours in Christ Jesus, who, though He was in the form of God, did not count equality with God a thing to be grasped, but emptied Himself, by taking the form of a servant, being born in the likeness of men. And being found in human form, He humbled Himself by becoming obedient to the point of death, even death on a cross" (Philippians 2:3–8). Showing and sharing God's love in Christ Jesus is the strongest thing you can do.

FAITH NOTES

To whom do you need to show love to right now? Write their names below.

....

....

....

....

....

....

....

....

....

7

WHAT IT MEANS TO BE A MAN: DENY YOURSELF

ONE-SENTENCE DEVOTION

Through His radical and brave self-sacrifice on the cross, Jesus revealed God's new direction for a successful life: deny yourself, take up your cross, and follow Him.

GOD'S WORD SPEAKS

Then Jesus told His disciples, "If anyone would come after Me, let him deny himself and take up his cross and follow Me. For whoever would save his life will lose it, but whoever loses his life for My sake will find it." (MATTHEW 16:24–25)

NEED A LITTLE MORE?

The message you receive from the world is to take care of yourself and do what makes you happy. Jesus calls you to a better life through His grace. He calls you to deny yourself, embrace the suffering that comes with that denial, and follow His pathway of complete self-sacrifice for others. It's easy to be all about yourself. It's easy to do what makes you happy, spend money on yourself, put yourself first, and build yourself up by putting other people down. That's our default as sinners. There's no effort required. But to be brave, to be strong and courageous, and to give up your own preferences and needs so others can be served is possible only through the gift of new life in Jesus. Just before Jesus was arrested in the Garden of Gethsemane, He told Peter, "Put your sword into its sheath; shall I not drink the cup that the Father has given Me?" (John 18:11). This is the life given through Baptism—the courageous life of putting others first. It's what makes you a real man.

FAITH NOTES

Whom do you need to serve these days?

8

WHAT IT MEANS TO BE A MAN: SAVED BY GRACE

ONE-SENTENCE DEVOTION

You have been saved from death, rescued from never being enough, and forgiven for your failures and sins, all out of God's unconditional love for you, which was earned by Jesus on the cross and delivered to you through God's Word, the gift of Baptism, and the blessing of Holy Communion.

GOD'S WORD SPEAKS

Jesus called them to Him and said, "You know that the rulers of the Gentiles lord it over them, and their great ones exercise authority over them. It shall not be so among you. But whoever would be great among you must be your servant, and whoever would be first among you must be your slave, even as the Son of Man came not to be served but to serve, and to give His life as a ransom for many." (MATTHEW 20:25–28)

NEED A LITTLE MORE?

Instead of walking away from you when you fail, don't measure up, or do something embarrassing, Jesus draws closer to you to help and save you. Instead of laughing at you when you are down or mocking you in your weakness, Jesus frees you from being a prisoner of sadness, sin, and hopelessness. This is a gift of God—not something you earn or deserve. God's help and forgiveness are given completely because of His grace. The Bible declares, "For by grace you have been saved through faith. And this is not your own doing; it is the gift of God, not a result of works, so that no one may boast" (Ephesians 2:8–9). This is the most important news you will ever receive and is the essential foundation for your life as a man, now and forever.

FAITH NOTES

Confess your faith today with the words of the Apostles' Creed:

> I believe in God, the Father Almighty, maker of heaven and earth.
>
> And in Jesus Christ, His only Son, our Lord, who was conceived by the Holy Spirit, born of the virgin Mary, suffered under Pontius Pilate, was crucified, died and was buried. He descended into hell. The third day He rose again from the dead. He ascended into heaven and sits at the right hand of God the Father Almighty. From thence He will come to judge the living and the dead.
>
> I believe in the Holy Spirit, the holy Christian Church, the communion of saints, the forgiveness of sins, the resurrection of the body, and the life everlasting. Amen.

1

PURITY PATHWAY: YOU DON'T HAVE TO HIDE

ONE-SENTENCE DEVOTION

Life with God means you never have to hide, because even when you fail and even when you sin, God loves you, welcomes you, and calls you His own, allowing you to be free from secrets and shame.

GOD'S WORD SPEAKS

Again Jesus spoke to them, saying, "I am the light of the world. Whoever follows Me will not walk in darkness, but will have the light of life." (JOHN 8:12)

NEED A LITTLE MORE?

After Adam and Eve sinned, they hid from God in the Garden of Eden. They were ashamed of their disobedience and found themselves walking in darkness. Walking in darkness, concealing what you're doing, is a clear indicator of impurity in your life. What are you hiding? Are you lying to your parents about where you go, what you're doing, and who you're with? Do you immediately turn off your phone or close a browser when someone enters your room? Is your behavior with your girlfriend inappropriate for others to see? Walking in darkness means that you're not walking in Jesus' direction. But instead of a life in hiding, Jesus gives you a life in the light. If you practice appropriate public affection with your girlfriend, you don't have to hide. If your online activity can be viewed by all, you do not need to keep it secret. If you can speak the truth to your parents, you are on the path of purity. Even if you're hiding in darkness right now, Jesus loves you so much that He calls you out of secrecy, blesses you with His forgiveness, and leads you to a new start in His light today.

FAITH NOTES

What in your life needs to come out of darkness so that you can have forgiveness and renewal?

2

PURITY PATHWAY: KINDNESS FIRST

ONE-SENTENCE DEVOTION

While the world tempts you to act crudely toward girls, Jesus gives you a life shaped by His grace that leads you to do something much better: be kind, show respect, and give women the same grace the Lord gives you.

GOD'S WORD SPEAKS

[Jesus said,] "Blessed are the merciful, for they shall receive mercy." (MATTHEW 5:7)

NEED A LITTLE MORE?

How do you treat girls? You may think girls are impressed when you try to act cool or when you show off a buff body, talk tough, or control them. But think again. Girls want to meet boys who are kind and thoughtful and genuine. They would rather meet boys who have a great sense of humor than a big ego. God won us with His kindness, sending His Son to show God's great mercy and to earn our forgiveness, salvation, and eternal life through His death and resurrection. Kindness and mercy are the gifts given by God's grace to the world—and they're part of the guidance Jesus gives for treating women well.

FAITH NOTES

Practice being kind and respectful to a girl you like and to a girl who may not be included by others.

3

PURITY PATHWAY: TURN AWAY

ONE-SENTENCE DEVOTION

In addition to changing your actions with the gift of new life He won for you on the cross, Jesus also changes your heart, filling it with a new way of looking at women—not with lust, but with love and respect.

GOD'S WORD SPEAKS

[Jesus said,] "You have heard that it was said, 'You shall not commit adultery.' But I say to you that everyone who looks at a woman with lustful intent has already committed adultery with her in his heart." (MATTHEW 5:27–28)

NEED A LITTLE MORE?

Sometimes living a life of purity is as simple as turning your eyes away from temptation and turning off a device that is leading you to look at a woman lustfully. You get good at what you practice. If you practice turning your eyes away from what leads you toward impure thoughts, you will get good at it. If you cave in to an ongoing use of pornography or leering at women as sex objects, you will reinforce this impure behavior. The new heart Jesus gives you in Baptism causes you to look at women as wonderfully created and fellow redeemed children of God. Turn away from anything less. As the Bible says, "Whatever is true, whatever is honorable, whatever is just, whatever is pure, whatever is lovely, whatever is commendable, if there is any excellence, if there is anything worthy of praise, think about these things" (Philippians 4:8). You can admire a woman's beauty, but you should do it with respectful eyes and a pure heart.

FAITH NOTES

What impure online practice do you need to turn away from today?

4

PURITY PATHWAY: PROOF OF LOVE

ONE-SENTENCE DEVOTION

True love that would lead to a sexual relationship with a woman is proven when you give yourself to her in the commitment of marriage, just as God proved His love for us with the ultimate commitment: sending His Son to die for us, even in our sin (see Romans 5:8).

GOD'S WORD SPEAKS

[Jesus said,] "It was also said, 'Whoever divorces his wife, let him give her a certificate of divorce.' But I say to you that everyone who divorces his wife, except on the ground of sexual immorality, makes her commit adultery, and whoever marries a divorced woman commits adultery." (MATTHEW 5:31–32)

NEED A LITTLE MORE?

Marriage is a precious gift from God. It is a reflection of the relationship Jesus has with His people. The Bible calls Jesus the Bridegroom and His church the Bride. In earthly marriage, husbands love their wives as Christ loved the church (see Ephesians 5:25). This is a lifetime public commitment. Yet divorce happens. When it does, we rely on God's strength and forgiveness for those very difficult situations. But marriage is meant to last. Marriage makes a husband and wife "one flesh" (Ephesians 5:31). They share everything with each other. If you love a girl and she loves you, it doesn't mean you can have sex. That blessing is for a marriage commitment. Sex isn't an opportunity for your personal satisfaction. If you're not ready to marry a girl, you're not ready to have sex with her. Instead, you need to get to know her, become her friend, and take an interest. As you grow closer to her, she may let you show appropriate public signs of affection—like holding hands, hugging, and kissing. That's an exciting and fun blessing as you ask God to guide you to the girl who will become your wife. Then your physical bond can grow in marriage.

FAITH NOTES

Which couples in your life provide good examples of marriage? Note below the helpful qualities you see in their lives.

....

....

....

....

....

....

....

....

5

PURITY PATHWAY: WHAT COMES NATURALLY

ONE-SENTENCE DEVOTION

The natural and easy pathway of behaving badly, living immorally, and speaking crudely can only be broken by Jesus, who took all your sin upon Himself in order to create a new heart and spirit in you with His grace and truth.

GOD'S WORD SPEAKS

[Jesus said,] "For from within, out of the heart of man, come evil thoughts, sexual immorality, theft, murder, adultery, coveting, wickedness, deceit, sensuality, envy, slander, pride, foolishness. All these evil things come from within, and they defile a person." (MARK 7:21–23)

NEED A LITTLE MORE?

If you just go along with the crowd, you will most likely end up joining in the crude, rude, and disrespectful talk about girls and people who aren't "in the group." The crowd thinks this is funny and cool. The crowd makes you comfortable with cursing, swearing, and insults. All of that darkness flows naturally from a sinful heart. Jesus interrupted the natural flow of your heart by filling you with His Spirit. God's Word and the gift of Baptism drown the foul natural junk in your heart and give birth to a new heart with new words and attitudes. The Bible says, "The fruit of the Spirit is love, joy, peace, patience, kindness, goodness, faithfulness, gentleness, self-control" (Galatians 5:22–23). That's the goodness grown by the Spirit of Jesus in you. Why settle for what comes naturally when you can live and speak in ways that bless and build up the people around you?

FAITH NOTES

Read this verse and think about how you can lead the crowd instead of following it:

Let no corrupting talk come out of your mouths, but only such as is good for building up, as fits the occasion, that it may give grace to those who hear. (Ephesians 4:29)

6

PURITY PATHWAY: FILLED WITH GOOD THINGS

ONE-SENTENCE DEVOTION

Jesus fills you with God's goodness so it overflows from your life to others, but an empty life—without a regular diet of God's Word—becomes a breeding ground for bad behavior.

GOD'S WORD SPEAKS

[Jesus said,] "When the unclean spirit has gone out of a person, it passes through waterless places seeking rest, and finding none it says, 'I will return to my house from which I came.' And when it comes, it finds the house swept and put in order. Then it goes and brings seven other spirits more evil than itself, and they enter and dwell there. And the last state of that person is worse than the first." (LUKE 11:24–26)

NEED A LITTLE MORE?

Jesus delivers you from evil. The Holy Spirit crowds out junk from your mind and heart. All good things come from God (see James 1:17). But if you fill your mind with horror movies, your heart with sexual impurity, your reflexes with violent video games, and your psyche with social media snark, you can expect a cauldron of anxious and shaken thoughts and feelings to boil inside you. You won't feel very good, and you'll probably act poorly. The question to ask yourself every day is this: "What's filling me up?" Junk will bring you down, but God's Word will fill you with goodness, hope, wisdom, and strength. Hanging with friends who help you follow Jesus' guidance will encourage you. Worshiping God, receiving Holy Communion, remembering your Baptism, and thanking Him for His blessings through His sacrifice on the cross for you will give you peace. If you start to feel down, ask yourself what's filling you up. Then be filled with God's good things.

FAITH NOTES

Write down what makes you feel anxious, sad, or angry. How can you replace those things with God's goodness and gifts?

7

PURITY PATHWAY: THE PURPOSE OF SEX

ONE-SENTENCE DEVOTION

God created the sexual relationship between a husband and wife who are married to reflect His intimate and self-sacrificial relationship with us, to create new human beings, and to bless a marriage with selfless and joyful love.

GOD'S WORD SPEAKS

[Jesus said,] "It is written, 'My house shall be a house of prayer,' but you have made it a den of robbers." (LUKE 19:46)

NEED A LITTLE MORE?

Everything God created has a purpose. When people turned the temple into a sales center, Jesus stepped in to restore it as God's house of prayer. Your body is God's temple too. The Bible says, "Or do you not know that your body is a temple of the Holy Spirit within you, whom you have from God? You are not your own, for you were bought with a price. So glorify God in your body" (1 Corinthians 6:19–20). The purpose of your body is to point to God's goodness, purity, and love as you care for it and use it. God created sex as a gift for a husband and wife in marriage so it can reflect the amazing intimate relationship God has with us, create new human beings who can know God's love, and provide a way for a husbands and wives to show selfless love to each other. As a young man, you need to take the lead in respecting girls—not pressuring them into sex—and wait to bless your wife with a sexual relationship when you get married. Your self-control and respect will bless the girls in your life, glorify God, and prepare you well for marriage.

FAITH NOTES

Write goals for how you will treat girls well and how you will prepare to be a good husband one day.

8

PURITY PATHWAY: WATCH OUT!

ONE-SENTENCE DEVOTION

Because Jesus gives you genuine rest and refreshment—walking with you always—you don't need to obey the deceiving voices that tempt you to escape into substance abuse, self-harm, or acting out.

GOD'S WORD SPEAKS

Jesus answered them, "See that no one leads you astray. For many will come in My name, saying, 'I am the Christ,' and they will lead many astray." (MATTHEW 24:4–5)

NEED A LITTLE MORE?

Watch out! Be careful! There are voices in the world, and even in your head, that will tell you the only way to rest and find relief is to escape—escape through anger, alcohol, tobacco, drugs, sex, running away, or self-harm. Jesus warned you that many would try to take His place as the source of rest and relief. Don't believe those voices that lead you to the wide road of self-destruction. Jesus brings you the true source of restoration. He said, "Come to Me, all who labor and are heavy laden, and I will give you rest" (Matthew 11:28). When you are weary, frustrated, or worried, go to Him in prayer. Cast your cares upon Him, because He cares for you (see 1 Peter 5:7). Hear His promises in His living Word. Because of God's kindness to you, shown so clearly in His sending His Son to be your Savior and friend, you have the ultimate resource for rest and refreshment. You can be confident that your Good Shepherd will restore your soul (see Psalm 23:3). You can also know that even Jesus is praying for you when you face challenges and trouble: "Christ Jesus is the one who died—more than that, who was raised—who is at the right hand of God, who indeed is interceding for us" (Romans 8:34).

FAITH NOTES

Try writing a song that expresses the pathway of Jesus' purity below. Post it on social media.

....

....

....

....

....

....

....

....

....

1

RELATIONSHIP 101: LOVE ONE ANOTHER

ONE-SENTENCE DEVOTION

Live so that the way you treat others in every relationship comes from the way Jesus treats you: with love, by giving you life, and by being a blessing.

GOD'S WORD SPEAKS

[Jesus quoted Isaiah and said,] "The Spirit of the Lord is upon Me, because He has anointed Me to proclaim good news to the poor. He has sent Me to proclaim liberty to the captives and recovering of sight to the blind, to set at liberty those who are oppressed." (LUKE 4:18)

NEED A LITTLE MORE?

In every relationship, your goal is not to see what you can get out of people. It is to give. God placed you in your family, in friendships, and in romantic relationships to show His self-sacrificial love. You are there to be an encourager, a healer, and someone who brings goodness and blessing. You're not there to insist on your way, to loudly voice your opinion, or to have everyone in your life serve you for your maximum pleasure. You're there to show God's love. Jesus said, "These things I command you, so that you will love one another" (John 15:17). You do this because you were first loved by God, who sent His Son to save you and give you life. If you travel this path of being a servant and loving people in your life, you will have healthy relationships and grateful loved ones. You'll also see that when two people in a relationship give themselves fully to each other, both receive what they need.

FAITH NOTES

Experiment with active listening: listen to truly understand and receive information, not to give your reply. Ask follow-up questions so you can understand what someone is saying and so you can hear all the details of his or her story. Don't share about yourself or give your opinion unless you're asked. See how this makes the other person feel.

2

RELATIONSHIP 101: HOW TO TREAT A GIRL

ONE-SENTENCE DEVOTION

If you like a girl and are truly interested in getting to know her, approach her with the pure heart given to you by God's grace through Jesus, not with the intent of using her or treating her meanly.

GOD'S WORD SPEAKS

[Jesus said,] "Blessed are the pure in heart, for they shall see God." (MATTHEW 5:8)

NEED A LITTLE MORE?

Important tip: sending a girl a crude meme or putting something gross in her locker at school will not make her like you. The heart of a healthy relationship is kindness. God revealed that secret when He sent the world His kindness in Jesus, whose ultimate act of love was taking the world's sins to the cross. Power, control, and pestering do not win someone's heart. In fact, power is a lazy substitute for showing Jesus' love. If you want to impress a girl, be kind to her, talk to her, and ask her about things she likes. Get to know her story. Listen to her. Look her in her eyes. Stand up for her. Be a friend. It takes more courage to be kind than to look cool. Girls aren't looking for the coolest or strongest guy with the best clothes and perfect hair. They're looking for a nice guy with a pure heart. That's who Jesus shapes you to be.

FAITH NOTES

Watch other guys to see how they treat girls.
Write some dos and don'ts below.

DOS	DON'TS
....	....
....	....
....	....
....	....
....	....
....	....
....	....
....	....
....	....
....	....
....	....
....	....
....	....
....	....
....	....

3

RELATIONSHIP 101: HOW TO FORGIVE

ONE-SENTENCE DEVOTION

God gives you a place where you can release your hurts and truly forgive people in your life; this place is called the cross, where Jesus carried sin and wrong that would otherwise crush you and separate you from God.

GOD'S WORD SPEAKS

Then Peter came up and said to [Jesus], "Lord, how often will my brother sin against me, and I forgive him? As many as seven times?" Jesus said to him, "I do not say to you seven times, but seventy-seven times." (MATTHEW 18:21–22)

NEED A LITTLE MORE?

How do you forgive someone? When you're wounded by someone's wrong, you may not feel like forgiving that person. You may feel like getting revenge, cutting the person from your life, or ghosting him or her. Getting hurt hurts—a lot. The answer to your pain is in the word *forgiveness*. It means "to let go." Your first step in forgiveness is to release your pain to the One who carried all your pain on the cross and conquered it when He rose from the dead. You can't handle your hurt, but Jesus can, did, and will. Give it to Him. When it starts to overwhelm your heart or dominate your mind, say, "Take my pain, dear Jesus. Carry it for me because it's too much for me to bear." Keep giving your wounds to the One who was wounded for your peace and restoration. Next, if it's possible and if it's the right time, seek reconciliation with the person who wounded you. Listen, talk, apologize, and let healing begin. Release the wrong from your relationship so you can be restored in your love and care for each other. Forgiveness will lift you up and bless others.

FAITH NOTES

Practice giving your hurt to God and living in His peace.

4

RELATIONSHIP 101: GIVE PEOPLE A CHANCE

ONE-SENTENCE DEVOTION

Sometimes you feel like rushing to judge people in order to make yourself feel better, but because Jesus called you His own even when you were dead in sin, your faith life means patiently giving people a chance.

GOD'S WORD SPEAKS

[Jesus said,] "Why do you see the speck that is in your brother's eye, but do not notice the log that is in your own eye?" (MATTHEW 7:3)

NEED A LITTLE MORE?

You may have heard the saying "Don't judge a book by its cover." That's what this verse is talking about. Instead of condemning you, the Bible says, "God shows His love for us in that while we were still sinners, Christ died for us" (Romans 5:8). You now share that mercy and grace with people in your life. When you humbly recognize your imperfections and flaws—the log in your own eye—you can be patient and show kindness to others. You don't rush to judgment. You don't pick on the weak and unpopular or harbor hatred toward the beautiful and well-liked or the people who don't think like you do. You get to know people's stories. You love because God first loved you (see 1 John 4:19). You give people a chance.

FAITH NOTES

Say hello and start a conversation with someone you wouldn't normally talk to at school, work, or church.

5

RELATIONSHIP 101: BOUNDARIES

ONE-SENTENCE DEVOTION

People will try to pull you into their arguments and bad behavior, but Jesus puts you in relationships so you can share the love and kindness He has given you.

GOD'S WORD SPEAKS

[Jesus said,] "Do not give dogs what is holy, and do not throw your pearls before pigs, lest they trample them underfoot and turn to attack you." (MATTHEW 7:6)

NEED A LITTLE MORE?

Someone once said, "If you wrestle with a pig, both of you will get muddy, but only the pig will enjoy it." In other words, don't get pulled into someone else's drama. "Friends" will try to lure you into their wrong behavior. People will try to drag you into their meaningless arguments. Bullies will try to make you behave like they do. Don't join the trouble or hurt. God called you His own in Baptism and sent you into the world to bring His new life to people, not so you would simply follow the crowd or blend in. Knowing Jesus gives you boundaries that keep you out of the "mud pit" for your own well-being and guide you toward the fruit of the Holy Spirit: "love, joy, peace, patience, kindness, goodness, faithfulness, gentleness, and self-control" (Galatians 5:22–23). In Christ, your Savior from sin and an example for how to have good relationships, you are a person who resists the temptation to imitate negativity and unkindness.

FAITH NOTES

Read the fruit of the Holy Spirit in Galatians 5.
Circle the fruit that you need most right now.

But the fruit of the Spirit is love, joy, peace, patience, kindness, goodness, faithfulness, gentleness, self-control; against such things there is no law. And those who belong to Christ Jesus have crucified the flesh with its passions and desires. (Galatians 5:22–24)

6

RELATIONSHIP 101: PROBLEM-SOLVING

ONE-SENTENCE DEVOTION

When you run into issues or problems with someone, approach him or her with the same love and patience Jesus shows you: go to the person to speak kindly and gently about the issue and be willing to make more than one attempt to settle things peacefully.

GOD'S WORD SPEAKS

[Jesus said,] "If your brother sins against you, go and tell him his fault, between you and him alone. If he listens to you, you have gained your brother." (MATTHEW 18:15)

NEED A LITTLE MORE?

If someone offends you, you may feel like spreading rumors about how bad he or she is. If you run into a relationship problem, you may feel like talking about it to everyone except the person involved. As sinners, we're afraid to face issues. As fragile people, we don't like the pressure, tension, and discomfort brought on by conflict. But no matter how you feel, the way to a peaceful and healthy relationship does not involve gossip, slander, insults, or avoidance. You will decrease the baggage, guilt, and denial in your life if you simply swallow hard and settle issues face to face. You may need a little time to prayerfully calm down and get ready. But at the right time, set up a time to talk. Don't accuse. Instead, talk about how you felt then and how you feel now. Make it your problem as much as it is anyone else's. Then ask, "How can we make this better?" Take the journey of forgiveness and reconciliation. That's the journey Jesus took to put you right with God. It's a relationship pathway that will bless you and the people in your life.

FAITH NOTES

Practice saying you're sorry. Write what you're sorry for. Then pray for the courage and opportunities to ask for forgiveness from the appropriate people.

7

RELATIONSHIP 101: PRACTICE SERVING OTHERS

ONE-SENTENCE DEVOTION

Jesus set the course for happy and healthy relationships: people serving one another as He served us and gave His life for us.

GOD'S WORD SPEAKS

[Jesus said,] "For even the Son of Man came not to be served but to serve, and to give His life as a ransom for many." (MARK 10:45)

NEED A LITTLE MORE?

It is very easy to make life all about yourself. "Me, me, me" is what you have thought since you were an infant. But it is also your sinful default: me first, others next. Becoming self-sacrificial depends on God's course correction and takes lots of practice. God turned you away from self-centeredness when He sent His Son to give His life for you. Jesus gives you His selfless mind and heart. Jesus guides you to "do nothing from selfish ambition or conceit, but in humility count others more significant than yourselves" (Philippians 2:3). Every day, you are called to practice this new life. You think before you speak. You don't dominate conversations or clamor for attention. You watch out for others and defend the weak. You practice thoughtfulness to loved ones and strangers. You give the benefit of the doubt, brush off small annoyances, and explain things in the kindest way. You're present for friends and family. You practice, practice, practice serving because the servant Son of God continues to serve you every day.

FAITH NOTES

If someone is really bothering you, how can you brush it off and show kindness?

8

RELATIONSHIP 101: YOU ARE LOVED

ONE-SENTENCE DEVOTION

The tools, confidence, and fulfillment you need for every relationship you ever have are always rooted in the perfect, generous, loving, and life-building relationship God has established with you through His Son, Jesus.

GOD'S WORD SPEAKS

And twisting together a crown of thorns, they put it on His head and put a reed in His right hand. And kneeling before Him, they mocked Him, saying, "Hail, King of the Jews!" And they spit on Him and took the reed and struck Him on the head. And when they had mocked Him, they stripped Him of the robe and put His own clothes on Him and led Him away to crucify Him. (MATTHEW 27:29–31)

NEED A LITTLE MORE?

The Gospel changes everything. The Good News of Jesus' life, death, and resurrection for you sets you on a new pathway in life. Being baptized into Christ and having His Word in your life fills every situation with hope and lifts you up with God's grace in every time of need. Instead of condemning you because of your shortcomings, failures, and sins, God condemned His perfect Son. He was mocked, beaten, and nailed to the cross so you would never have to be stuck in shame, guilt, or hopelessness. God put His Son in the position of losing everything and suffering what you deserved so He would see you as pure, righteous, and good. Because Jesus took your place, God rejoices over you as His perfect child. That's what it means to be justified and redeemed. God's love for you is not because of what you achieve or how great you are—it is because you are wrapped with Jesus' righteousness and grace. God is merciful to you. He is kind. He loves you. That gift is the key to how you live in relationship with others. God's grace is where you begin.

FAITH NOTES

Write a song that covers what healthy relationships look like because of God's love. Post it on social media so others can hear the Good News.

1

BODY TIP: ONE OF A KIND

ONE-SENTENCE DEVOTION

Jesus has a body like you do, so He understands what it means to grow up and be human, and He helps you accept who you are physically (God's unique creation) so you can use your body to serve God and others.

GOD'S WORD SPEAKS

The Word became flesh and dwelt among us, and we have seen His glory, glory as of the only Son from the Father, full of grace and truth. (JOHN 1:14)

NEED A LITTLE MORE?

Jesus really understands you. He gets all the things that have to do with your body: your height, weight, build, physical strength, hair and eye color, complexion, and facial features. Jesus was a unique human being who grew up and used His physical self to accomplish God's mission of salvation. God created you as a unique physical being too. Your body is precious to Him—even with its quirks and peculiarities. What about the struggles or doubts you have about your body? The Bible gives great counsel: "For we do not have a high priest who is unable to sympathize with our weaknesses, but one who in every respect has been tempted as we are, yet without sin. Let us then with confidence draw near to the throne of grace, that we may receive mercy and find grace to help in time of need" (Hebrews 4:15–16). Jesus understands body issues and will help you as you struggle. But remember, God delights in you as a one-of-a-kind creation who blesses Him and others in a one-of-a-kind way.

FAITH NOTES

Ask your mom or dad which of your physical features she or he likes most.

2

BODY TIP: SMELL GOOD

ONE-SENTENCE DEVOTION

You are God's unique and loved creation, so caring for yourself with regular showers and deodorant keeps you smelling good and always ready to be close to others with help and friendship.

GOD'S WORD SPEAKS

All things were made through Him, and without Him was not any thing made that was made. (JOHN 1:3)

NEED A LITTLE MORE?

You are a precious and unique creation of God. He crafted you in love. You are irreplaceable. There's only one you. Do you know what that means? Maintenance. Yes, you need to take care of the one-of-a-kind treasure called "you." Caring for the gifts in your life is called "stewardship." Just as you are on this earth to be a steward of creation, of your possessions, and of other people, you are also on this earth to take care of yourself. What does that mean? Take a shower every day. Yes. Every. Day.

With soap. Maybe more often if you're lifting weights, playing ball, or going on a run. It also means brushing your teeth and using deodorant. Yes, put it on. What about cologne? Go easy on the fragrances. Smell nice, but don't smell nice in the next county. Take the initiative to take care of the gift of your physical self. Don't depend on your mom and dad to bug you about keeping clean. Take ownership of maintaining your body. You are a precious creation of God, who loves you and gave His life for you. Your body is a vessel to communicate that love. Care for it well.

FAITH NOTES

Thank God for your body—yes, the way it is. As you read the following Bible verse, write down two or three habits that can help you glorify God with your body.

Or do you not know that your body is a temple of the Holy Spirit within you, whom you have from God? You are not your own, for you were bought with a price. So glorify God in your body. (1 Corinthians 6:19–20)

3

BODY TIP: GATEKEEPING

ONE-SENTENCE DEVOTION

As your Creator and Savior, Jesus cares about your body and entrusts you with the work of caring for it well—from what you eat to healthy activity levels to guarding yourself from damage done by smoking, drinking alcohol, and using drugs.

GOD'S WORD SPEAKS

Now when the sun was setting, all those who had any who were sick with various diseases brought them to [Jesus], and He laid His hands on every one of them and healed them. And demons also came out of many, crying, "You are the Son of God!" But He rebuked them and would not allow them to speak, because they knew that He was the Christ. (LUKE 4:40–41)

NEED A LITTLE MORE?

Jesus has a physical body—even at this moment. After His resurrection, He showed His scars to His disciples and had meals with them. During His life on earth, He healed and cared for ailing bodies wherever He went.

Your body is a precious gift. It is part of who you are. That's why you're called to take care of this blessing from God. Not every food item is perfectly healthy, but some will keep you healthier than others. You may not become a professional athlete, but physical activity will keep your body strong. You may not be able to stay completely unaffected by damaging substances, but you can resist getting caught up in smoking, drinking alcohol, and using drugs. You are the gatekeeper for what happens to your body. Steward your physical self well. By doing so, you honor God, who created you, and the Savior, who gave His body for your eternal life.

FAITH NOTES

How can you improve the way you care for yourself?

4

BODY TIP: EXERCISE

ONE-SENTENCE DEVOTION

As Jesus was a physical man, frequently on the move to visit people and share the Good News of God's love and forgiveness, you also were created to be active, exercising your body and taking part in sharing God's love.

GOD'S WORD SPEAKS

[Jesus] said to them, "I must preach the good news of the kingdom of God to the other towns as well; for I was sent for this purpose." (LUKE 4:43)

NEED A LITTLE MORE?

Jesus really got around. He went to a lot of places and met a lot of people. When Jesus wanted to go somewhere, He walked. By this, you can see that you were made to move. Physical activity is really good for you. If you get into the habit of regular movement and exercise, you will see the benefits for years to come. You'll be a healthy son, a healthy friend, and, one day, a healthy husband, father, and grandfather. Keep moving and, as you connect with lots of people, keep sharing Jesus' love and hope and promise of salvation.

FAITH NOTES

How many hours each day do you devote to movement and exercise? Note one way you can improve your physical activity.

5

BODY TIP: SLEEP

ONE-SENTENCE DEVOTION

Your body needs a healthy rhythm of activity and rest; that's how God created you, and that's why Jesus took breaks and even invited His disciples to rest when their schedule became too hectic.

GOD'S WORD SPEAKS

[Jesus] said to them, "Come away by yourselves to a desolate place and rest a while." (MARK 6:31)

NEED A LITTLE MORE?

You require a lot of sleep. Yes, even more than eight hours sometimes. Your body is growing and needs sleep to pump out those growth hormones. Rest is important. It's so important that God established a rhythm of work and rest for His people. After God freed the people of Israel from a life of constant slavery, He gave them a day of rest: "Remember the Sabbath day, to keep it holy. Six days you shall labor, and do all your work, but the seventh day is a Sabbath to the LORD your God. On it you shall not do any work" (Exodus 20:8–10). Even Jesus took time out of His schedule as the Savior of the world to sleep (see Matthew 8:24). The life Jesus guides you through is not a one-dimensional, fear-of-missing-out, you-only-live-once, high-intensity existence. It is a sustainable and healthy life with a time and season for everything (see Ecclesiastes 3:1–8)—rest and sleep included—for a lifetime of service to God.

FAITH NOTES

Are you getting your eight hours? Note what sleep improvements may help your health and energy levels.

6

BODY TIP: HELP FOR HEALTH

ONE-SENTENCE DEVOTION

You can ask Jesus to help you when you struggle with your health and wellness; He cares about your physical well-being.

GOD'S WORD SPEAKS

And behold, there was a woman who had had a disabling spirit for eighteen years. She was bent over and could not fully straighten herself. When Jesus saw her, He called her over and said to her, "Woman, you are freed from your disability." And He laid His hands on her, and immediately she was made straight, and she glorified God. (LUKE 13:11–13)

NEED A LITTLE MORE?

Maybe you blew out your knee playing a sport. Perhaps you were born with a health issue that has required surgery or daily medication or some sort of device. You may be limited in where you can go or what you can eat because of asthma or allergies. Health challenges are hard. But if there's one thing the accounts of Jesus' life in the Gospels makes clear, it's that Jesus came to heal and restore. He responds to your requests for physical help. It may be through a doctor or with the assistance of medicine. It may be through an answer to prayer. It may be by giving you patience and using your experience to bless and encourage others. Your body might not be perfected until you're in heaven, but trust that Jesus cares about you and invites you to share your troubles with Him to receive His help in your time of need.

FAITH NOTES

Pray for a person you know who is experiencing illness or physical difficulty.

7

BODY TIP: ACCEPT YOURSELF

ONE-SENTENCE DEVOTION

The quest for more can be distracting and destructive—more muscles, better abs, thinner, bulkier, bigger, leaner—which is why celebrating your identity as a beloved child of God just the way you are is the path Jesus puts you on by His grace.

GOD'S WORD SPEAKS

Jesus, seeing that he had become sad, said, "How difficult it is for those who have wealth to enter the kingdom of God! For it is easier for a camel to go through the eye of a needle than for a rich person to enter the kingdom of God." (LUKE 18:24–25)

NEED A LITTLE MORE?

Jesus spoke to a rich ruler in Luke 18. This man was distracted by his wealth. It separated him from the life of contentment and peace Jesus graciously gave. The same could be true if you're seeking the perfect body. Media inundates you with lean, cut, and low-percentage-body-fat images with rippling abs and popping pecs. Those bodies are oiled and posed to highlight every muscular contour. The images are edited and unrealistic. If that is the ideal you're supposed to strive for, you're in for a frustrating quest. You're also being set up for despising your own body. If your body image is taking hits because you feel like you can never be good enough, something is very wrong. So listen carefully: Jesus created you. He gave His life for you—yes, even for your body. What the world says is never enough, Jesus celebrates. Of course, it's good to take care of yourself, but if your drive to be in shape is preventing you from accepting yourself, you need to pause and hear the affirming word of God from David: "For You formed my inward parts; You knitted me together in my mother's womb. I praise You, for I am fearfully and wonderfully made" (Psalm 139:13–14).

FAITH NOTES

Thank God for your body. Tell Him what makes you uniquely you.

8

BODY TIP: GETTING OLD

ONE-SENTENCE DEVOTION

This side of heaven, your body will falter and decline, but God gives you His lasting Word and the gift of eternal life to bring you enduring hope and strength.

GOD'S WORD SPEAKS

[Jesus said,] "Heaven and earth will pass away, but My words will not pass away." (MATTHEW 24:35)

NEED A LITTLE MORE?

Statistics show that you will reach your physical peak at about thirty-five years old. After that, your body begins to decline. You won't be as fast. You won't be as strong. You won't even be able to think as quickly as you do now. Your reflexes will slow down. In this fallen and sin-broken world, your body is part of that damaged reality. You will get old, and your body will fail. The Bible says, "The years of our life are seventy, or even by reason of strength eighty; yet their span is but toil and trouble; they are soon gone, and we fly away" (Psalm 90:10). That's why idolizing your body is misguided. You need to care for it, but your physical self can't be the center of your existence. You need more than just exercise, workouts, nutrition, and sports. You need God's enduring Word. You need His everlasting presence in the Sacraments (Baptism and the Lord's Supper). You need the eternal life He gives. Who you are is more than skin deep. Your life is shaped by God's meaningful Word and life-giving gifts.

FAITH NOTES

Write a Bible verse that is important to you below.

1

WWW.REALITY

ONE-SENTENCE DEVOTION

Before you get lost in the virtual world, you need to know that God loves you in the real world, draws close to you with His real Word and presence, and gives you the great purpose of showing His love and sharing His Good News with real people.

GOD'S WORD SPEAKS

[Zechariah said,] "Because of the tender mercy of our God, whereby the sunrise shall visit us from on high to give light to those who sit in darkness and in the shadow of death, to guide our feet into the way of peace." (LUKE 1:78–79)

NEED A LITTLE MORE?

Beware of getting lost in the gaming universe or the fake world of social media. It's very easy to get stuck doomscrolling, to forget to eat or sleep, or to put off going to the bathroom as you conquer the next video game obstacle with your friends online. Remember that there is a real world out there. There are real people. God sent His "sunrise" from on high, Jesus, the Savior, to shine His light to everyone sitting in the darkness and shadows. Knowing this real light and truth is really important before you enter the virtual world. When you understand God's love for you and are tuned in to His purpose for you, you can build virtual gaming and viewing habits that give priority to real people and the real purpose of shining Jesus' light.

FAITH NOTES

When do you disconnect so you can experience the real world?

2

WWW.KINDNESS

ONE-SENTENCE DEVOTION

Jesus, who is the light of the world (see John 8:12), fills you with His light so that you are a light that radiates His goodness, kindness, love, and new life to everyone in your life—including your life online.

GOD'S WORD SPEAKS

[Jesus said,] "You are the light of the world. A city set on a hill cannot be hidden. Nor do people light a lamp and put it under a basket, but on a stand, and it gives light to all in the house. In the same way, let your light shine before others, so that they may see your good works and give glory to your Father who is in heaven." (MATTHEW 5:14–16)

NEED A LITTLE MORE?

Social media and online connections have opened the door to snarkiness, bullying, and careless sharing. It's easier to be mean when you can't be seen. It's tempting to be thoughtless or cruel when you can react quickly with a few taps of the screen. But God's will for your worldwide impact is not your own self-promotion.

Having friends and followers for the purpose of building yourself up and tearing others down is harmful to everyone. Your purpose is to share God's kindness and to shine the light of Jesus' love. You're saved by God's grace, which means you, a Christian gentleman, have the opportunity to show grace to others. Your politeness and respect for others needs to be reflected in your posts. And language? Your clean and caring words will point people to the goodness of God. You don't need to post everything, but when you do appear online, you are the light of the world, shining Jesus' love and care.

FAITH NOTES

Post something today that shines Jesus' light.

3

WWW.INFLUENCER

ONE-SENTENCE DEVOTION

Just as God planned to rescue you from sin, death, and hopelessness through His Son, Christ Jesus, your online purpose is to influence people for Christ's Gospel so they can receive the most important gift in the world—eternal life with Him.

GOD'S WORD SPEAKS

Jesus said to Simon, "Do not be afraid; from now on you will be catching men." And when they had brought their boats to land, they left everything and followed Him. (LUKE 5:10–11)

NEED A LITTLE MORE?

Yes, you are a social media influencer. We've all become that to a degree. The question is, how are you influencing others? Are you setting an example of carelessness, meanness, and crude language? Are you blending in with a life centered on materialism, sports, or crazy memes? Or do you have a plan to bless people with what is most important in life: the Good News that Jesus loves them, hears their prayers, died to forgive their sins, and rose to give them the gift of eternal life? Remember that in the middle of all the things you want to do online, your ultimate purpose is to influence others with the blessing of the meaningful and eternal life given by Jesus.

FAITH NOTES

Write your plan to shine Jesus' light on your social media, gaming, and any other your online platforms below.

4

WWW.SCORPIONS

ONE-SENTENCE DEVOTION

God promises to give you what nourishes and blesses you; but be careful, for while the virtual world promises pleasure, it often gives you stinging poison.

GOD'S WORD SPEAKS

[Jesus said,] "What father among you, if his son asks for a fish, will instead of a fish give him a serpent; or if he asks for an egg, will give him a scorpion? If you then, who are evil, know how to give good gifts to your children, how much more will the heavenly Father give the Holy Spirit to those who ask Him!" (LUKE 11:11–13)

NEED A LITTLE MORE?

Look up from your screens to see the beauty of God's creation. Put your phone down to notice the blessing of the people in your life. Lift up your head to soak in the abundance of God's gifts and gracious activity for you—unlimited forgiveness, grace, and mercy through Jesus. Take a rest from the two-dimensional world to be bathed with real 3D wonder. And be careful. The world will try to tell you that its virtual portal will make you happier, more connected, and more significant. But that's a lie. While connecting to the metaverse can be helpful and entertaining, it will often end up stinging you with poisonous comments, ensnaring you with pornographic obsessions, and immobilizing you with endless scrolling. God is the one who really cares about you and fills your life with His outstretched arms of salvation. Use virtual connections as a tool to accomplish your plans; don't let the scorpions of online domination poison God's purpose for you.

FAITH NOTES

Who in your life can help you stay accountable for what you access online and how often you are connected?

5

WWW.LEGACY

ONE-SENTENCE DEVOTION

While Jesus gives you what is truly important—His love, hope, strength, and eternal life—He also comforts you with the fact that avoiding some online trends will make you a better person, not someone who is missing out or behind the times.

GOD'S WORD SPEAKS

[Jesus said,] "Woe to the world for temptations to sin! For it is necessary that temptations come, but woe to the one by whom the temptation comes! And if your hand or your foot causes you to sin, cut it off and throw it away. It is better for you to enter life crippled or lame than with two hands or two feet to be thrown into the eternal fire. And if your eye causes you to sin, tear it out and throw it away. It is better for you to enter life with one eye than with two eyes to be thrown into the hell of fire." (MATTHEW 18:7–9)

NEED A LITTLE MORE?

Your virtual life is filled with temptation. You feel the pressure to join the latest trends or to comment on the most current argument. But remember, what you do digitally sticks around—and sticks to you—for a long time. It's better to cut off your connection to all that is foul and destructive than to become a minion of the ugly cyberworld. Jesus spoke dramatically about losing limbs rather than being lost in hell. Your faith life leads you to curate your online legacy well and wisely—even if it means severing your participation in what is damaging and demonic.

FAITH NOTES

Write a plan for what you want your cyber imprint to look like when you are thirty years old.

6

WWW.SUSPICION

ONE-SENTENCE DEVOTION

God gives wisdom and understanding that keep you from being taken in by the wicked and deceptive schemes rampant in the cyberworld, so be watchful and have a healthy suspicion about what comes your way electronically.

GOD'S WORD SPEAKS

[Jesus said,] "The master commended the dishonest manager for his shrewdness. For the sons of this world are more shrewd in dealing with their own generation than the sons of light." (LUKE 16:8)

NEED A LITTLE MORE?

Jesus told a parable about a desperate manager who figured out how to survive after he was fired. The manager was clever—more shrewd than some people who walked with God! Being shrewd about the ways of the world is important. Having a healthy suspicion about what comes your way electronically is essential. That post, that message, that website—it may be a big lie.

Proverbs 2:6–7 says, “For the Lord gives wisdom; from His mouth come knowledge and understanding; He stores up sound wisdom for the upright; He is a shield to those who walk in integrity.” Don’t believe everything that comes at you. Have a healthy and wise suspicion. Let God’s understanding and insight be your shield in the cyberworld. And ask the Holy Spirit to help you be a good manager of your time and abilities. After all, our true treasure is not in this world; it’s in the world to come that Jesus promises to all who believe in Him.

FAITH NOTES

What steps do you take if you suspect some eworld fakery or phishing?

7

WWW.LOOK_UP

ONE-SENTENCE DEVOTION

If you're in the habit of looking down at screens, posts, messages, and updates that disconnect you from mental and emotional contact with others, remember that God gives you something refreshing and renewing: He lifts your head to see Him, His salvation, and His invitation to see and love the people around you.

GOD'S WORD SPEAKS

[Jesus said,] "And then they will see the Son of Man coming in a cloud with power and great glory. Now when these things begin to take place, straighten up and raise your heads, because your redemption is drawing near." (LUKE 21:27–28)

NEED A LITTLE MORE?

You may have grown up with a tablet or phone in front of you at all times: videos to keep you occupied on road trips, games to entertain you at church, activities to fill the time during family visits, even homework to supplement what you do in school. You may be so accustomed to keeping your head down and your eyes on a screen that not looking at a device makes you feel like something is missing. But hear this news flash: an overdose of screen time and virtual living can cause you to miss real life and ruin relationships. If you go out with a girl, she would love for you to take an interest in her and look into her eyes rather than check your phone every sixteen seconds or watch the television in the restaurant. The God who sees you gives you the gift of seeing people. The God who saves you gives you the gift of lifting up your head to see the help He provides. Your faith life is not a heads-down existence. As the Bible says, "I lift up my eyes to the hills. From where does my help come? My help comes from the LORD, who made heaven and earth" (Psalm 121:1–2). God gives you the gift of looking up to see a full life in Him and with others.

FAITH NOTES

Try not to look at a screen for one day this week.
How did it change your life that day?

....

....

....

....

....

....

....

....

8

WWW.FORGIVENESS

ONE-SENTENCE DEVOTION

Living in an ever-changing world of technology is so difficult, complicated, and challenging that you will inevitably make mistakes and stumble into failure, but Jesus catches you in the safety net of forgiveness and restoration, plugging you into His grace and love and removing the heavy weight of virtual pressure and confusion.

GOD'S WORD SPEAKS

[Jesus said,] "But watch yourselves lest your hearts be weighed down with dissipation and drunkenness and cares of this life, and that day come upon you suddenly like a trap." (LUKE 21:34)

NEED A LITTLE MORE?

Technology is a great blessing, but it can also set you up for some bad mistakes. No doubt, there are already times you have failed in your online life. You said mean things. You accessed a really bad site. You were deceptive. You fell for a scam. The consequences are so much bigger and much more public than messing up in the privacy of your own home. How can you make it through the scandal and sin? The answer is forgiveness—real and complete forgiveness from God Himself. The stain you think is absolutely unable to be cleaned is washed as white as snow through the blood of Jesus (see Isaiah 1:18)—blood spilled as He took all the grief, pain, and consequences for your wrongs. In Christ, you are forgiven. His Word delivers it to your life. Baptism washes you clean. When God looks at you, He sees someone who gets an award for complete goodness. Yes, that's you. It's you because all your online sins were nailed to the cross. The weight is removed. Today, God gives you a new beginning.

FAITH NOTES

Ask God to forgive you for one of your failures. Let Him know what your new life will look like.

....

....

....

....

....

....

....

....

....

....

1

MIND AND HEART: TRUTH

ONE-SENTENCE DEVOTION

You need a solid, intellectual foundation of truth in your life, which is what God gives you in His Word.

GOD'S WORD SPEAKS

Inasmuch as many have undertaken to compile a narrative of the things that have been accomplished among us, just as those who from the beginning were eyewitnesses and ministers of the word have delivered them to us, it seemed good to me also, having followed all things closely for some time past, to write an orderly account for you, most excellent Theophilus, that you may have certainty concerning the things you have been taught. (LUKE 1:1–4)

NEED A LITTLE MORE?

Doubters abound everywhere you go. Critics question everything. Skeptics cast doubt on everyone. Sometimes their voices are so loud and they get so much attention that you begin to believe them. You even lose confidence in God and His Word. But think again. As Luke noted in the opening to his Gospel, he conducted research with eyewitnesses. He examined firsthand accounts and put together a solid historical narrative. And it wasn't just Luke. The Bible is the most well-documented manuscript in history. In addition to its airtight accuracy, the Bible presents deep and abiding truth—answers to the questions of our hearts and souls and wisdom that defies anything humans have ever come up with. You need a solid foundation of truth for every intellectual judgment. That's what God gives you in His Word: the truth of who Jesus is and what He does for you. The truth is, Jesus is the foundation of your life.

FAITH NOTES

How are you doing on your Bible-reading plan? (See pp. 31 and 63 for reminders on how to get started.)

2

MIND AND HEART: BALANCE

ONE-SENTENCE DEVOTION

God created you to be a well-balanced person who serves Him and others with your heart, soul, mind, and strength—that's the gift of a life that balances brain power with love, faith, and service.

GOD'S WORD SPEAKS

When [Jesus] went ashore He saw a great crowd, and He had compassion on them and healed their sick. (MATTHEW 14:14)

NEED A LITTLE MORE?

During this stage of life, your brain gets a lot of emphasis. You're in school almost every day. Parents and teachers push you to think, think, think. That's a good thing. It's important to learn. Your brain is in prime condition to retain lots of good and helpful things. But God created you to be more than just a walking brain. Your heart, soul, and actions are important too. When Jesus saw crowds of people who were in need, He felt compassion and responded with healing help. God created emotions. Your life is a balance of thoughts, feelings, and actions. The Bible says, "For with the heart one believes and is justified, and with the mouth one confesses and is saved" (Romans 10:10). Knowing that you are Jesus' beloved child is more than an intellectual truth; it is a heart relationship with your Savior, who loves you. It is faith and trust in God, who calls you His own and saves you. It is confessing Him through words and actions that share His love. God gives you the gift of balance by providing your heart, soul, mind, and strength to bless others.

FAITH NOTES

List what makes you feel the following emotions.

Sad: ....

....

Mad: ....

....

Glad: ....

....

Scared: ....

....

3

MIND AND HEART: THE PURPOSE OF KNOWLEDGE

ONE-SENTENCE DEVOTION

Learning things isn't for the purpose of becoming arrogant, self-centered, or better than others; it is to grow as someone who can build people up and bless the world—always serving the one who really knows all things, the almighty God, your Savior.

GOD'S WORD SPEAKS

And behold, there arose a great storm on the sea, so that the boat was being swamped by the waves; but He was asleep. And they went and woke Him, saying, "Save us, Lord; we are perishing." And He said to them, "Why are you afraid, O you of little faith?" Then He rose and rebuked the winds and the sea, and there was a great calm. And the men marveled, saying, "What sort of man is this, that even winds and sea obey Him?" (MATTHEW 8:24–27)

NEED A LITTLE MORE?

Many of the disciples were expert fishermen and seafarers. They understood how to handle a boat in any weather. But the storm recorded in Matthew 8 got the best of them. It was too big, too strong, and too rough. All they could do was panic and cry out to Jesus for help. How did Jesus respond? He spoke a word and calmed the storm. Jesus showed the disciples that their knowledge was limited. So is yours. You may know a lot, but God knows everything. As Romans 11:33 says, "Oh, the depth of the riches and wisdom and knowledge of God! How unsearchable are His judgments and how inscrutable His ways!" God didn't give you brain power so you can become a know-it-all filled with arrogance about everything you've learned. Your knowledge is a gift from God to build people up and to bring blessing to the world. "'Knowledge' puffs up, but love builds up" (1 Corinthians 8:1). Let God's love for you guide what you do with your knowledge.

FAITH NOTES

What is your favorite subject in school? How can your love for that subject bring blessings to others?

4

MIND AND HEART: ANGER

ONE-SENTENCE DEVOTION

Sometimes you will feel angry, but in the same way that Jesus' anger led Him to correct what was wrong and to bring salvation to the lost, your anger is meant to be used for good and not for harm.

GOD'S WORD SPEAKS

The Passover of the Jews was at hand, and Jesus went up to Jerusalem. In the temple He found those who were selling oxen and sheep and pigeons, and the money-changers sitting there. And making a whip of cords, He drove them all out of the temple, with the sheep and oxen. And He poured out the coins of the money-changers and overturned their tables. And He told those who sold the pigeons, "Take these things away; do not make My Father's house a house of trade." His disciples remembered that it was written, "Zeal for Your house will consume Me." (JOHN 2:13–17)

NEED A LITTLE MORE?

What gets you angry? Jesus didn't want His Father's house, the temple in Jerusalem, to become a place where greedy vendors made their profits. The temple was supposed to be a place of prayer. So Jesus threw out the swindlers and sellers. Anger is an important feeling. It can push you to defend others and do the right thing, but it can also push you over the edge. You need to be careful with anger. The Bible says, "Be angry, and do not sin; ponder in your own hearts on your beds, and be silent. Offer right sacrifices, and put your trust in the LORD" (Psalm 4:4–5). When you become swept up by anger, feel it but don't act out. Stop, pause, and pray. Sliding into a sinful reaction may hurt you and others. Most of the time, anger needs to be pondered in silence so your next steps reflect trust in your Savior. And remember this: Jesus has already been judged and has paid the price for all the sin and wrongdoing in the world. When God looks at you, it's with love because Jesus has you covered.

FAITH NOTES

List some helpful responses and some hurtful responses when you get angry.

....

....

....

....

5

MIND AND HEART: JOY

ONE-SENTENCE DEVOTION

Jesus is joyful about you, His loved and forgiven child; that's why you can celebrate His happiness by being happy and joyful about His blessings and not always take yourself so seriously.

GOD'S WORD SPEAKS

[Jesus said,] "What man of you, having a hundred sheep, if he has lost one of them, does not leave the ninety-nine in the open country, and go after the one that is lost, until he finds it? And when he has found it, he lays it on his shoulders, rejoicing. And when he comes home, he calls together his friends and his neighbors, saying to them, 'Rejoice with me, for I have found my sheep that was lost.' Just so, I tell you, there will be more joy in heaven over one sinner who repents than over ninety-nine righteous persons who need no repentance." (LUKE 15:4–7)

NEED A LITTLE MORE?

Do you like to laugh? Who doesn't like humor and fun? God created laughter and joy. Feelings of delight make you feel better. And sometimes things strike you as funny. When Sarah was told she would have a baby in her old age, she laughed (see Genesis 18:10–12). When God brought His people out of captivity, they said, "Then our mouth was filled with laughter, and our tongue with shouts of joy" (Psalm 126:2). Jesus said there is joy in heaven when a sinner repents—when someone who is lost is found. Life is filled with serious things, but there are times when you need to celebrate. Joy shows that troubles are only temporary in the presence of God's lasting love, so take a break from taking yourself and life so seriously. God's precious children can have a good laugh and live with joy in the knowledge that Jesus, our Good Shepherd, rejoices because we are His.

FAITH NOTES

See if you can make someone laugh today.

6

MIND AND HEART: COMPARISON

ONE-SENTENCE DEVOTION

Jesus releases you from getting stuck in the comparison vortex by filling your heart and mind with contentment and gratitude; that's why you don't need to be consumed with complaints when your life isn't going the way you think it should.

GOD'S WORD SPEAKS

Jesus said to [the rich young man], "If you would be perfect, go, sell what you possess and give to the poor, and you will have treasure in heaven; and come, follow Me." When the young man heard this he went away sorrowful, for he had great possessions. (MATTHEW 19:21–22)

NEED A LITTLE MORE?

It's so easy to get stuck making comparisons—being unhappy with what you don't have instead of being grateful for what you do have. You can fill every day with grumbling as you lay your life next to someone else's and think that person is doing better than you. But making comparisons will send you into a never-ending spiral of dissatisfaction. You'll never be happy if you always look around at everyone else. Jesus tried to release the rich young man from his slavery to stuff and status, but the young man was stuck. You don't have to be. When Jesus died for you, He earned the riches of God's grace for your life. As your Savior walks with you, He breaks the mind loop of grumbling and replaces it with gratitude. He gives you the gift of contentment to replace complaint.

FAITH NOTES

When people complained about who Jesus was and what He was teaching, Jesus answered them, "Do not grumble among yourselves" (John 6:43). What are you most tempted to grumble about? How can you give thanks to God instead?

7

MIND AND HEART: SADNESS

ONE-SENTENCE DEVOTION

Sometimes you need to be sad, you need to cry, and you need to rest in Jesus' comforting embrace.

GOD'S WORD SPEAKS

Jesus wept. (JOHN 11:35)

NEED A LITTLE MORE?

When Jesus' friend Lazarus died, Jesus was really sad. He felt His own loss and pain and that of His friends and Lazarus's sisters. He cried. Tears flowed. It wasn't the only time Jesus cried. When Jesus arrived in Jerusalem and saw Mary weeping, He wept because He realized God's people wouldn't recognize that He was their Savior. Jesus experienced sadness. So do you. When your heart is grieved or broken, when you suffer loss and pain, you need to cry. You need to be sad when sad things happen. It's healthy to release your emotions and feel your sorrow. You may not want to be a sniffling mess, but sadness is an expression of love. When tears flow, look to the promise of restoration that God provides in His beloved Son. The Bible says, "The Lord GOD will wipe away tears from all faces" (Isaiah 25:8). Yes, one day, sadness will be gone, and your heart will be healed.

FAITH NOTES

What is making you sad these days?

8

MIND AND HEART: HABITS

ONE-SENTENCE DEVOTION

If you go through life focusing on hopelessness and bad things, you will get very good at being hopeless and filled with dread, but your risen Savior, Jesus, gives you better habits: faith-filled confidence and relief-providing prayer.

GOD'S WORD SPEAKS

Now after the Sabbath, toward the dawn of the first day of the week, Mary Magdalene and the other Mary went to see the tomb. And behold, there was a great earthquake, for an angel of the Lord descended from heaven and came and rolled back the stone and sat on it. His appearance was like lightning, and his clothing white as snow. And for fear of him the guards trembled and became like dead men. But the angel said to the women, "Do not be afraid, for I know that you seek Jesus who was crucified. He is not here, for He has risen, as He said. Come, see the place where He lay. Then go quickly and tell His disciples that He has risen from the dead, and behold, He is going before you to Galilee; there you will see Him. See, I have told you." So they departed quickly from the tomb with fear and great joy, and ran to tell His disciples. And behold, Jesus met them and said, "Greetings!" And they came up and took hold of His feet and worshiped Him. Then Jesus said to them, "Do not be afraid; go and tell My brothers to go to Galilee, and there they will see Me." (MATTHEW 28:1–10)

NEED A LITTLE MORE?

The habits you establish now will become what you get good at for the rest of your life. If you practice living as if the weight of the world rests on your shoulders, you will become skilled at worry, anxiety, negativity, and panic. But God doesn't give you that kind of life. Jesus rose from the dead and gave you a life built on His resurrection. You are baptized, born anew, and you have certain hope for an eternal future. Your new habits are hope, prayer, courage in Christ, and service to others. You live a life of faith that will carry you through whatever life throws at you.

FAITH NOTES

The Bible says to "pray without ceasing" (1 Thessalonians 5:17). Every day, all the time, you can talk to God like He's a friend standing next to you. Two important parts of prayer are saying thank You and asking for help. Write some prayers for each category in a journal or on a separate piece of paper.

Thank You, God, for . . .

Help me, God, with . . .

1

GROWING IN FAITH: THE MAIN THING

ONE-SENTENCE DEVOTION

God loves you so much that He sent Jesus to live a perfect life for you, carry all your burdens and sins, die in your place, rise from the dead to defeat death, and give you forgiveness and life so His peace, joy, and eternal hope can live in you and be given to others through you by the work of the Holy Spirit.

GOD'S WORD SPEAKS

"Behold, the virgin shall conceive and bear a son, and they shall call His name Immanuel" (which means, God with us). (MATTHEW 1:23)

NEED A LITTLE MORE?

God's grace is your key to life. Even though you're a sinner, even though the world is fallen, and even though you feel the pain of life's brokenness, God loves you, saves you, and gives you everything you need to live in Him with purpose and peace forever. God lavished you with His love even though you don't deserve it and didn't earn it. When God looks at you, He sees the perfection and goodness of Jesus because you have been clothed with Christ through Baptism (see Galatians 3:27). Jesus was forsaken by God as He hung on the cross and cried out, "My God, My God, why have You forsaken Me?" (Matthew 27:46). He suffered this fate so you would never have to. The Bible says, "With His wounds we are healed" (Isaiah 53:5). God's grace in your life through Jesus is the main thing. It's what you live by. It's what sustains you in every aspect of your journey through life.

God delivers His grace to you through the Word, Baptism, and Holy Communion. It's what lives through you to do good and bless the world.

FAITH NOTES

Draw what comes to mind when you think of God's grace.

2

GROWING IN FAITH: WORSHIP

ONE-SENTENCE DEVOTION

When you see how much God loves you and all He has done for you, you fall down to worship Him with your whole life with fellow believers in your church and throughout the world.

GOD'S WORD SPEAKS

And going into the house, [the Wise Men] saw the child with Mary His mother, and they fell down and worshiped Him. Then, opening their treasures, they offered Him gifts, gold and frankincense and myrrh. (MATTHEW 2:11)

NEED A LITTLE MORE?

Going to church is really important. In the company of fellow believers, you humble yourself before God, receive His gifts, and thank Him for His goodness. Worship acknowledges that your life is not your own. It is a gift from your gracious Savior-God. The Magi—or Wise Men—found the child Jesus and bowed down before Him in worship. They presented Him with precious gifts. That's the consistent picture of worship in the Bible. Bowing down acknowledges that God is in charge, that He comes to you with His grace and salvation, and that He is the one who is faithful and reliable. Then you respond to His goodness with a complete life of thanks and praise. Going to church cultivates a life of worship—a life that depends on Jesus and serves Him. Church resets your life from serving yourself to seeing your Savior. You need this grace-filled reset regularly. It's the same approach to life taken by some very wise men.

FAITH NOTES

If you've not been going to church regularly, start up the weekly habit. If you do go to church regularly, note one takeaway each week that steers your life toward serving Jesus.

3

GROWING IN FAITH: WHO'S IN CHARGE?

ONE-SENTENCE DEVOTION

Jesus leads the way in your life with His Word, His ways, and His wisdom as you follow Him with gratitude and trust His plan instead of yours.

GOD'S WORD SPEAKS

Jesus said to [the devil], "Again it is written, 'You shall not put the Lord your God to the test.'" (MATTHEW 4:7)

NEED A LITTLE MORE?

The devil tried to call the shots when He tempted Jesus. The evil one asserted his agenda, attempting to lure Jesus into following a twisted plan of power, pleasure, and ego. But, unlike Adam and Eve in the Garden of Eden, Jesus didn't fall for Satan's deception. Jesus stayed on the narrow road of sacrificing His life for the sins of the world. Intent on giving His life for yours, Jesus said, "Be gone, Satan! For it is written, 'You shall worship the Lord your God and Him only shall you serve'" (Matthew 4:10). Sometimes you want to make Jesus follow you and conform to your plans. But it's good that He's in charge. Jesus gives you what you really need: a new life and eternal hope, courage and strength to meet each day, and purpose and character to bless the world. Jesus is not a divine vending machine or your assistant coach. He is in front, charting the course with His grace and wisdom for your life. Follow Him and worship Him alone.

FAITH NOTES

What request has Jesus told you no to? Talk to Him in prayer about giving you patience and acceptance.

4

GROWING IN FAITH: HOW TO PRAY

ONE-SENTENCE DEVOTION

God gives you the gift of prayer—conversation with Him anytime and anywhere—just as if He is one of your friends standing next to you.

GOD'S WORD SPEAKS

[Jesus said,] "When you pray, you must not be like the hypocrites. For they love to stand and pray in the synagogues and at the street corners, that they may be seen by others. Truly, I say to you, they have received their reward. But when you pray, go into your room and shut the door and pray to your Father who is in secret. And your Father who sees in secret will reward you." (MATTHEW 6:5–6)

NEED A LITTLE MORE?

Prayer is an amazing gift from God. God invites you to put all your troubles and anxieties on His shoulders (see Psalm 55:22). Jesus gives you access to God. When you pray in Jesus' name, you acknowledge that He is the way to the Father. As your Advocate, Jesus promises that your prayers are heard. Therefore, because Jesus takes away your sin (which is the barrier between you and God), God hears your prayers and responds (see Psalm 50:15). He challenges you to stick with prayer and not give up (see Luke 18:1). And He promises to answer you when you ask, seek, and knock (see Matthew 7:7–8). God speaks to you in His Word. As you hear Him, He wants to hear your thoughts, questions, needs, reasons for gratitude, and requests (see Philippians 4:6). Prayer connects you with God, who has the power to help you overcome your problems. In addition to formal prayers before meals, at bedtime, and at church, make your thought-life a conversation with God. Instead of worrying, complaining, wishing, or grumbling, bring everything and everyone to God in constant prayer. Your Father in heaven is eager to hear and help you.

FAITH NOTES

Do you know the Lord's Prayer? It's what Jesus taught His disciples in Matthew 6:9–13. You can learn it and pray it the way the Christian Church has prayed it for centuries:

> Our Father who art in heaven, hallowed be Thy name, Thy Kingdom come, Thy will be done on earth as it is in heaven; give us this day our daily bread; and forgive us our trespasses as we forgive those who trespass against us; and lead us not into temptation, but deliver us from evil. For Thine is the kingdom and the power and the glory forever and ever. Amen.

5

GROWING IN FAITH: NO-SHOW

ONE-SENTENCE DEVOTION

Living a Christian life is not about establishing a public platform or becoming a famous leader, preacher, or teacher; it is about being led by Jesus on a distinct pathway of His choosing, receiving His love and forgiveness, and blessing and lifting up others with His gifts.

GOD'S WORD SPEAKS

[Jesus said,] "And when you fast, do not look gloomy like the hypocrites, for they disfigure their faces that their fasting may be seen by others. Truly, I say to you, they have received their reward. But when you fast, anoint your head and wash your face, that your fasting may not be seen by others but by your Father who is in secret. And your Father who sees in secret will reward you." (MATTHEW 6:16–18)

NEED A LITTLE MORE?

Fasting is when you give up eating—or something in your diet—for a short time so your hunger and discomfort can remind you of Jesus' suffering for you and His sacrifice for your sin. People have been doing this for a long time. Back in Jesus' day, He reminded people that fasting was not done to get attention and gain sympathy. It was a quiet and personal journey of devotion to God. That's true of your faith. You're not a Christian so you can be famous and popular—the coolest member of the youth group, the best musician, the most melodic singer, or the greatest leader. Your faith is about Jesus for you. You were dead in sin, but He gave you the gift of life. Now you humbly go where Jesus sends you and see how He chooses to shine through you—as you suffer or as you succeed. You're not a Christian to be in the limelight. You're a Christian so you can point to Jesus, the light of life.

FAITH NOTES

Do you try to be the center of attention? How can you replace those attempts with pointing people to Jesus?

6

GROWING IN FAITH: IDOLS

ONE-SENTENCE DEVOTION

One of the most dangerous traps in life is becoming obsessed with an idol—anything that captivates you and controls your life, replacing your faithful Savior and Friend, Jesus, and leading you in a direction that will fade and fail.

GOD'S WORD SPEAKS

[Jesus said,] "No one can serve two masters, for either he will hate the one and love the other, or he will be devoted to the one and despise the other. You cannot serve God and money." (MATTHEW 6:24)

NEED A LITTLE MORE?

Money is a popular idol. Some people live to get more money. There are many other possible idols, including appearance, friends, parties, gaming, sports, girls, popularity, hunting, clothes, and being right (feel free to add to the list). The apostle John summed up idol categories when he said, "For all that is in the world—the desires of the flesh and the desires of the eyes and pride of life—is not from the Father but is from the world" (1 John 2:16). Chasing those worldly idols will drain you and never satisfy you. Idols lead you away from Jesus, who gives you life, prepares your purpose, and supplies all you need. Jesus gives the best so the best can be first in your life. Jesus said, "But seek first the kingdom of God and His righteousness, and all these things will be added to you" (Matthew 6:33). You never lose out when you walk in the life given to you by Jesus. It's nice to enjoy life's blessings, but idols can't compare to the ultimate blessing of life in Christ, your Savior.

FAITH NOTES

Draw your biggest idol temptation. Then write out Matthew 6:33 right through it.

7

GROWING IN FAITH: ARMOR

ONE-SENTENCE DEVOTION

Life on this side of heaven is not easy—a spiritual battle is raging as evil tries to win the day and destroy you—but Jesus won the victory through the cross and grave, and He is the one who equips you and fights for you.

GOD'S WORD SPEAKS

[Jesus] put another parable before them, saying, "The kingdom of heaven may be compared to a man who sowed good seed in his field, while his men were sleeping, his enemy came and sowed weeds among the wheat and went away. So when the plants came up and bore grain, then the weeds appeared also. And the servants of the master of the house came and said to him, 'Master, did you not sow good seed in your field? How then does it have weeds?' He said to them, 'An enemy has done this.' So the servants said to him, 'Then do you want us to go and gather them?' But he said, 'No, lest in gathering the weeds you root up the wheat along with them. Let both grow together until the harvest, and at harvest time I will tell the reapers, "Gather the weeds first and bind them in bundles to be burned, but gather the wheat into my barn."'" (MATTHEW 13:24–30)

NEED A LITTLE MORE?

Why is there so much evil in the world? The enemy, the devil, plants evil everywhere. You contribute, as well, with your fallen thoughts, words, and deeds. When will evil end? At the right time—but not before God completes His plan of salvation. Until that time, you are given spiritual armor to fight the good fight of faith. Ephesians 6:13–18 tells you how God outfits you: "Therefore take up the whole armor of God, that you may be able to withstand in the evil day, and having done all, to stand firm. Stand therefore, having fastened on the belt of truth, and having put on the breastplate of righteousness, and, as shoes for your feet, having put on the readiness given by the gospel of peace. In all circumstances take up the shield of faith, with which you can extinguish all the flaming darts of the evil one; and take the helmet of salvation, and the sword of the Spirit, which is the word of God, praying at all times in the Spirit, with all prayer and supplication." God's Word dresses you in this armor so you can be ready for the battle against the ways of the world.

FAITH NOTES

Read Ephesians 6:13–18 again. What armor are you most thankful for? Why? Write your answer in a journal or on another piece of paper.

8

GROWING IN FAITH: GIVING BACK

ONE-SENTENCE DEVOTION

God blessed you with the life-transforming gifts of forgiveness and eternal salvation—with that full life and with a grateful heart, you can joyfully be generous to others, sharing God's blessings and His Good News through your words, actions, and resources.

GOD'S WORD SPEAKS

[Jesus said,] "Give, and it will be given to you. Good measure, pressed down, shaken together, running over, will be put into your lap. For with the measure you use it will be measured back to you." (LUKE 6:38)

NEED A LITTLE MORE?

God's love and His gift of eternal life will last longer than a multibillion-dollar fortune, an all-star sports career, a record-breaking social media following, and high-profile Hollywood fame. Jesus gives you His priceless and endless gifts of forgiveness, strength, eternal hope, sustaining peace, and uplifting joy. He gives so much that it overflows from your life so you can give too. This is called stewardship—sharing what you've been given and using your talents and possessions to bless the world for God's glory. You can't outgive God. He keeps pouring on His blessing as you share with others. Before Jesus ascended into heaven, He said, "All authority in heaven and on earth has been given to Me. Go therefore and make disciples of all nations, baptizing them in the name of the Father and of the Son and of the Holy Spirit, teaching them to observe all that I have commanded you. And behold, I am with you always, to the end of the age" (Matthew 28:18–20). That passage is called "the Great Commission"—Jesus' words that lead you to share confidently and give back generously.

FAITH NOTES

How is gratitude to God being expressed in your generosity?

1

FRIENDS: THE FRIEND

ONE-SENTENCE DEVOTION

Jesus calls you His friend, and He proved His friendship by laying down His life to save you, which is your foundation for forging true friendships with others by loving the people in your life as your Savior has loved you.

GOD'S WORD SPEAKS

[Jesus said,] "This is My commandment, that you love one another as I have loved you. Greater love has no one than this, that someone lay down his life for his friends. You are My friends if you do what I command you. No longer do I call you servants, for the servant does not know what his master is doing; but I have called you friends, for all that I have heard from My Father I have made known to you." (JOHN 15:12–15)

NEED A LITTLE MORE?

In order to have friends, you need to know what a true friend is. Jesus set the standard when He befriended you—a fallen sinner with many shortcomings—by giving His life for you. Because you have already received His love and grace, you now follow Him on the path of true friendship. You show your friendship with Jesus by doing what He commands. You listen, learn, serve, and praise Him. You spend time with Him in worship, prayer, and the reading of His Word. You also follow in His steps by befriending others with caring, patient, forgiving, unconditional love. You become a friend like Jesus. And when you feel grouchy, lose your temper, show some unkindness, and fall short, your friend, Jesus, restores you and renews you so you can reflect Him to others again. If you ever feel alone, know that you have the greatest friend with you: Jesus, who is always by your side and who teaches you how to be a friend to others.

FAITH NOTES

What friend qualities do you see in Jesus? Who in your life needs to receive those blessings from you?

....
....
....
....
....
....
....
....
....
....
....

2

FRIENDS: BEWARE OF THE VORTEX

ONE-SENTENCE DEVOTION

Jesus carefully chose the people He hung out with, not allowing others to pull Him away from God's will and plan—this is the care and caution He gives you as you choose who you hang out with.

GOD'S WORD SPEAKS

[Jesus said,] "Beware of false prophets, who come to you in sheep's clothing but inwardly are ravenous wolves. You will recognize them by their fruits. Are grapes gathered from thornbushes, or figs from thistles? So, every healthy tree bears good fruit, but the diseased tree bears bad fruit." (MATTHEW 7:15–17)

NEED A LITTLE MORE?

A wise person once said, "If someone shows you who they are, believe them the first time." Friends who speak crudely and behave badly can pull you into a vortex of thinking and behavior that hurts you and others. Beware of the wolves that want your life to be eaten up by their appetite for trouble and destruction. You don't need to go there. It's no mystery who these friends are. Whether they are girls or guys, you can tell they're causing destruction in your life as clearly as you can tell the difference between growing good fruit or getting stuck by sharp thorns. Be discerning with friends. Don't get pulled into relationships that pull you away from God's plans and the goodness of Jesus' Gospel. Instead, hang out with Him in His Word and receive Him in the Lord's Supper when you go to church.

FAITH NOTES

Make a list of the kind of behaviors you don't want in your life.

3

FRIENDS: SENT

ONE-SENTENCE DEVOTION

When Jesus saves you and heals you from sin-stained despair, you are sent to show and share His goodness, restoration, and love with the people in your life—including the girls you date and the woman you will marry one day.

GOD'S WORD SPEAKS

As [Jesus] was getting into the boat, the man who had been possessed with demons begged Him that he might be with Him. And He did not permit him but said to him, "Go home to your friends and tell them how much the Lord has done for you, and how He has had mercy on you." And he went away and began to proclaim in the Decapolis how much Jesus had done for him, and everyone marveled. (MARK 5:18–20)

NEED A LITTLE MORE?

Talk about scary. Jesus encountered a strong man possessed by four thousand demons. The man was so strong that he couldn't be held by metal restraints. He had caused terror in a town for years. What did Jesus do? He confronted the demons and cast them into two thousand pigs. The pigs became crazed, ran down a hillside into the sea, and drowned. The demons were gone, and the man was restored. He sat clothed, calm, and convinced that Jesus was the person he wanted to follow. So he begged Jesus to let him come along. Instead, Jesus sent him to his friends. Jesus cared about the man's friends who lived in one of the most ungodly and lost regions of the area, the Decapolis. The Bible reading for today describes the amazing results. After giving you a life makeover with His grace, Jesus sends you too. As a young man, you need to remember that you are sent to be a true friend to others, including the girls you date and the woman you will marry one day. The foundation for your relationships with girls is friendship—not physical affection, looks, popularity, or money. You are sent to be a friend who shares Jesus' love, care, respect, and faith.

FAITH NOTES

What words and actions of friendship can you use to bless the girls you talk to?

....

....

....

....

....

....

4

FRIENDS: RESPONSIBILITY

ONE-SENTENCE DEVOTION

When He created you and redeemed you, God took responsibility for you; now He entrusts you, His saved servant, with the responsibility to show that love and care to the people in your life.

GOD'S WORD SPEAKS

[Jesus said,] "Everyone to whom much was given, of him much will be required, and from him to whom they entrusted much, they will demand the more." (LUKE 12:48)

NEED A LITTLE MORE?

What responsibilities do you have? Chores? Homework? A job? As you grow older, you become more responsible to and for people in your life. Family members and friends trust you to be careful and caring with your words and actions. If you hurt someone's feelings, you're expected to admit your fault, apologize, and change your behavior. Growing up means you need to think before you speak so you don't cause hurt in another person's heart. You are responsible for handling people with care. That's what Jesus did for you when He gave His life for you. Now, as a responsible and caring friend, you show His love to others (1 John 4:11).

FAITH NOTES

Who in your life might be helped or hurt by what you say and do? How can you be careful as you speak and act?

5

FRIENDS:
HOW MANY FRIENDS?

ONE-SENTENCE DEVOTION

Jesus knows YOUR name (see Isaiah 43:1), and He knit YOU together in your mother's womb (see Psalm 139:13)—that's the care and love that shape you, not merely for surface relationships with a big crowd, but also for the deep friendships you will have with certain people throughout your life.

GOD'S WORD SPEAKS

[Jesus said,] "Therefore the kingdom of heaven may be compared to a king who wished to settle accounts with his servants. When he began to settle, one was brought to him who owed him ten thousand talents. And since he could not pay, his master ordered him to be sold, with his wife and children and all that he had, and payment to be made. So the servant fell on his knees, imploring him, 'Have patience with me, and I will pay you everything.' And out of pity for him, the master of that servant released him and forgave him the debt. But when that same servant went out, he found one of his fellow servants who owed him a hundred denarii, and seizing him, he began to choke him, saying, 'Pay what you owe.' So his fellow servant fell down and pleaded with him, 'Have patience with me, and I will pay you.' He refused and went and put him in prison until he should pay the debt. When his fellow servants saw what had taken place, they were greatly distressed, and they went and reported to their master all that had taken place. Then his master summoned him and said to him, 'You wicked servant! I forgave you all that debt because you pleaded with me. And should not you have had mercy on your fellow servant, as I had mercy on you?'" (MATTHEW 18:23–33)

NEED A LITTLE MORE?

Did you notice the double standard in this parable? The man who was forgiven for so much debt wouldn't forgive someone else of a little loan. Having mercy on the people in your life reflects God's mercy for you and forges caring relationships with others. This takes time and effort. You may experience this kind of friendship with just a few people throughout your life. It's normal to have just one, two, or three deep and true friendships during your lifetime. You may not have met that friend yet. Be patient and practice being merciful and caring so you'll be ready to walk with a lifetime friend.

FAITH NOTES:

Do you have a close friend yet? Write that person's name in the margin of this page and say a prayer for your friend. If you haven't met a close friend yet, ask Jesus to prepare you for that person.

6

FRIENDS: ANNOYING

ONE-SENTENCE DEVOTION

Loving God and loving others sums up God's direction for your life because He loved you so much through His Son, which means you don't have to be annoying and confrontational with friends but can be caring, careful, and kind.

GOD'S WORD SPEAKS

And one of them, a lawyer, asked Him a question to test Him. "Teacher, which is the great commandment in the Law?" And He said to him, "You shall love the Lord your God with all your heart and with all your soul and with all your mind. This is the great and first commandment. And a second is like it: You shall love your neighbor as yourself. On these two commandments depend all the Law and the Prophets." (MATTHEW 22:35–40)

NEED A LITTLE MORE?

You may not realize it, but at your age and with all the energy you have, you may fall into the trap of being annoying. Yes, harassing friends, bothering girls, being loud, belching in public, passing gas noisily, turning up your music too loud, being messy with your things, and ignoring people can be very annoying. It's easy to become careless and loveless toward others. But now is the time to practice loving God and loving your neighbors—the people around you. Go to church. Listen to God's Word. Think before you act or speak. Pause to ponder if what you're about to do will truly express Jesus' love to the other person. If not, don't do it. It's better to be quiet, be still, and be considered a wise friend than to do something that is loveless or annoying.

FAITH NOTES

Read this verse and write how it might apply to you.

Even a fool who keeps silent is considered wise; when he closes his lips, he is deemed intelligent. (Proverbs 17:28)

7

FRIENDS: LOSING FRIENDS

ONE-SENTENCE DEVOTION

Just as people walked away from Jesus, you may lose friends who decide to follow a different path or go a different way in life; but through it all, Jesus will continue to walk with you.

GOD'S WORD SPEAKS

[Jesus said,] "Woe to you, scribes and Pharisees, hypocrites! For you clean the outside of the cup and the plate, but inside they are full of greed and self-indulgence. You blind Pharisee! First clean the inside of the cup and the plate, that the outside also may be clean." (MATTHEW 23:25–26)

NEED A LITTLE MORE?

Jesus was sad that His own people, the descendants of Abraham, turned from Him and persecuted Him. He even wept over the people in Jerusalem who wouldn't have faith in Him as God's Son and their Savior (Matthew 23:37). People turned away from Jesus. And people will turn away from you. That happens in life. You may lose friends as they change, develop new interests, or take different paths. It doesn't take away from the fun you had or the times you enjoyed, but it doesn't feel good. If you lose a friend or one fades from your life, give thanks for the good times you shared and ask God to help you move on to new friendships He has in store for you. Jesus will walk with you as friends come and go.

FAITH NOTES

If you're feeling sad about losing a friend, ask Jesus to comfort you as you grieve.

8

FRIENDS: THE BULLIED AND FORGOTTEN

ONE-SENTENCE DEVOTION

God cares for the weak, the unpopular, and the outcast—just as He reached you with His grace and salvation when you were lost in sin, and that's why your faith leads you to be compassionate and caring to the "least of these" (Matthew 25:40), the people around you who may be forgotten, overlooked, or lost.

GOD'S WORD SPEAKS

"For I was hungry and you gave Me food, I was thirsty and you gave Me drink, I was a stranger and you welcomed Me, I was naked and you clothed Me, I was sick and you visited Me, I was in prison and you came to Me." Then the righteous will answer Him, saying, "Lord, when did we see You hungry and feed You, or thirsty and give You drink? And when did we see You a stranger and welcome You, or naked and clothe You? And when did we see You sick or in prison and visit You?" And the King will answer them, "Truly, I say to you, as you did it to one of the least of these My brothers, you did it to Me." (MATTHEW 25:35–40)

NEED A LITTLE MORE?

Some kids are forgotten, made fun of, and even bullied. You may have experienced one of these scenarios. Or you may have been involved in picking on someone. Jesus noticed the people who were overlooked and outcast. He befriended them and helped them. That's what He did for you by coming to rescue you from sin and death. And that's the path He gives you to travel. It's better to walk in Jesus' path of kindness than to follow an unkind crowd. As God's precious child, you are here to befriend the weak, to be kind to the outcast, and to defend the bullied. You don't need to blend in with meanness; you are a new creation who sets the pace with Jesus' love.

FAITH NOTES

Who needs your friendship and kindness at school?

....

....

....

....

....

....

....

....

....

....

....

....

1 LOOKING AHEAD: YOUR FUTURE

ONE-SENTENCE DEVOTION

No one can tell you what your future will be, but Jesus lets you know how to travel into your life ahead with confidence and joy: He is the way.

GOD'S WORD SPEAKS

Jesus said to [Thomas], "I am the way, and the truth, and the life. No one comes to the Father except through Me." (JOHN 14:6)

NEED A LITTLE MORE?

You never know what the future holds, but Jesus knows what you need for every moment of what's coming in your life. You need Him. You need His Word of strength, the joy of forgiveness and salvation, the certainty of being His baptized child, the renewal of the Lord's Supper, and the lifeline of prayer. If you try to venture into the future on your own, you will face obstacles that will be impossible to overcome. With Jesus in your present and future, you will make it every step of the way.

FAITH NOTES

List your top three hopes for the future.

2

LOOKING AHEAD: YOUR HELPER

ONE-SENTENCE DEVOTION

You're not on a solo expedition on your trek into the future, because Jesus sent the Holy Spirit to help you, teach you, and give you peace for your journey forward.

GOD'S WORD SPEAKS

[Jesus said,] "And I will ask the Father, and He will give you another Helper, to be with you forever, even the Spirit of truth, whom the world cannot receive, because it neither sees Him nor knows Him. You know Him, for He dwells with you and will be in you." (JOHN 14:16–17)

NEED A LITTLE MORE?

The future may be a mystery, but it's not uncharted. Jesus holds the future in His hands and sends the Holy Spirit to guide you, help you, and teach you. The Spirit works through God's Word to give you what you need for your expedition into the days ahead. Jesus made this promise for your life: "But the Helper, the Holy Spirit, whom the Father will send in My name, He will teach you all things and bring to your remembrance all that I have said to you. Peace I leave with you; My peace I give to you. Not as the world gives do I give to you. Let not your hearts be troubled, neither let them be afraid" (John 14:26–27). You don't have to be afraid or anxious about your future. The Holy Spirit is your active Helper who will lead you with God's living and wise Word.

FAITH NOTES

What help do you need for the year ahead? How has Jesus provided for you in the past year?

3

LOOKING AHEAD: CHALLENGES

ONE-SENTENCE DEVOTION

God makes your heart right through the forgiveness and justification that come through Jesus, who also equips your heart to guide you as you travel on God's right path, even when you face challenges.

GOD'S WORD SPEAKS

[Jesus said,] "Blessed are those who are persecuted for righteousness' sake, for theirs is the kingdom of heaven." (MATTHEW 5:10)

NEED A LITTLE MORE?

Because of God's grace, your life is filled with God's righteousness, which is given to you and shining through you. As you move forward into the future, you will face challenges. You will be tempted to hurt people and to do things that may hurt yourself. You will be tempted to break the Ten Commandments and to break human laws. You will be tempted to disobey your parents and to shirk responsibilities. You will be among challenging people and in the middle of challenging situations. You will be tested and pressured. But for every temptation and challenge, God equips you with His righteousness. Clothed and covered with the new life Jesus earned on the cross, you are equipped to withstand life's challenges. Led by God's Word, which is a lamp to your feet and a light to your path (see Psalm 119:105), you travel safely, even through the muddy trail of persecution and pain.

FAITH NOTES

Do you know the Ten Commandments? (See Exodus 20:3–17.) Learn them by memory so you'll be equipped to face some future challenges.

1. You shall have no other gods.
2. You shall not misuse the name of the Lord your God.
3. Remember the Sabbath day by keeping it holy.
4. Honor your father and your mother.
5. You shall not murder.
6. You shall not commit adultery.
7. You shall not steal.
8. You shall not bear false witness against your neighbor.
9. You shall not covet your neighbor's house.
10. You shall not covet your neighbor's wife, or his male servant, or his female servant, or his ox, or his donkey, or anything that is your neighbor's.

4

LOOKING AHEAD: MOVING ON

ONE-SENTENCE DEVOTION

God gives you wisdom for the spiritual battle you face each day, but you will still encounter times when you need to walk away from situations or relationships that are not helpful or that you can't handle anymore; as God guides and leads, move on and trust Him to take care of such situations.

GOD'S WORD SPEAKS

[Jesus said,] "And if anyone will not receive you or listen to your words, shake off the dust from your feet when you leave that house or town." (MATTHEW 10:14)

NEED A LITTLE MORE?

Sometimes you need to move on. When a friendship isn't working or becomes harmful, you may need to admit that you can't fix it. You need to move on. When you're in a situation that you know won't go smoothly, you may need to accept the fact humbly that you can't make it any better. You need to move on. Whether you're involved in an activity, working at a job, experiencing a relationship, or being part of a group, there will be times when certain situations aren't working. Anxiety, arguments, personality differences, and unhappiness may signal that you need to step away and move on. If you're devoted to never quitting or have a huge sense of dedication and a massive work ethic, the Holy Spirit may have to make you very uncomfortable to let you know that it's time to move on. He'll do that. Don't miss the signals. Sometimes misery means you need to get counseling or help to improve the situation, but there are times when the situation won't work and won't get better. It may be time to commend it to God's care. You can trust that your Savior, who humbled Himself and made the ultimate sacrifice for you, will be with you when you have to humble yourself and move on.

FAITH NOTES

Is there anything you need to stop doing these days to allow room for the new thing God wants you to do?

5

LOOKING AHEAD: EVIL

ONE-SENTENCE DEVOTION

Evil will rage in this world until Jesus returns, but it cannot win, because of Jesus' death and resurrection; one day, sin and wickedness will be punished once and for all, so take heart when you struggle with evil, because God will make things right in the end.

GOD'S WORD SPEAKS

[Jesus said,] "Again, the kingdom of heaven is like a net that was thrown into the sea and gathered fish of every kind. When it was full, men drew it ashore and sat down and sorted the good into containers but threw away the bad. So it will be at the end of the age. The angels will come out and separate the evil from the righteous and throw them into the fiery furnace. In that place there will be weeping and gnashing of teeth." (MATTHEW 13:47–50)

NEED A LITTLE MORE?

Sometimes it seems like bad people get away with evil. Bullies walk away laughing, criminals avoid getting caught, and abusers slink off into the shadows. We can hope and expect that people who do wrong things will be held accountable, be moved to repentance, and be forgiven by Jesus the same way we are. But true evil—the kind that comes from the devil and that works to separate us from our Lord—has been defeated forever. The devil still lurks on earth in a continuous attempt to pull people away from God, but our Savior promises that in eternity, evil will be punished and destroyed. That's why the statement about "weeping and gnashing of teeth" is in the Bible. It's not because God is cruel or unfair; it's because God IS fair. With our confident faith in Jesus as our Savior, we can be certain that the punishment we deserved was put on Christ as He died on the cross. If anyone hangs onto his or her evil or persists in rejecting God's grace, God will put an end to that harmful evil once and for all. If you are tormented by evil, know that its days are numbered. God will make things right.

FAITH NOTES

Pray for people who keep doing evil and hurting others. Ask God to change their hearts and bring them to repentance.

6

LOOKING AHEAD: YOUR CAREER

ONE-SENTENCE DEVOTION

Jesus works blessing through every part of your life, so you can be confident with your career, even if it's not your favorite activity; Jesus can use all you do to bless others and shine His light.

GOD'S WORD SPEAKS

Now when it was evening, the disciples came to Him and said, "This is a desolate place, and the day is now over; send the crowds away to go into the villages and buy food for themselves." But Jesus said, "They need not go away; you give them something to eat." They said to Him, "We have only five loaves here and two fish." And He said, "Bring them here to Me." (MATTHEW 14:15–18)

NEED A LITTLE MORE?

As Jesus taught and healed a crowd that numbered five thousand families, it got very late, and the throng of people needed food. The disciples thought Jesus should solve the crisis, but Jesus told them that they should give the crowd something to eat. All they had were five loaves and two fish. What happened? "[Jesus] ordered the crowds to sit down on the grass, and taking the five loaves and the two fish, He looked up to heaven and said a blessing. Then He broke the loaves and gave them to the disciples, and the disciples gave them to the crowds. And they all ate and were satisfied. And they took up twelve baskets full of the broken pieces left over" (Matthew 14:19–20). Whatever small offering you bring to Jesus, He will multiply it and bless many people through it. You may find a career you love. Jesus can bless people through that line of work. You may end up in a career that isn't your favorite. But you can trust Jesus to work blessing even in a job that isn't ideal. If you work during your time in school, that time is used by Jesus to bless many too. Throughout your life, the jobs you work are more than jobs; they are ways to serve God and His people.

FAITH NOTES

How have you seen Jesus do something big with something small? Note any examples from your life so far.

....

....

....

....

....

....

....

7

LOOKING AHEAD: DECISIONS

ONE-SENTENCE DEVOTION

You are not alone as you face decisions, because the Holy Spirit will guide you, and God's Word will give you peace and direction; seek the Lord in prayer, read the Bible, and consult wise and godly people as you make decisions.

GOD'S WORD SPEAKS

And Peter answered Him, "Lord, if it is You, command me to come to You on the water." He said, "Come." So Peter got out of the boat and walked on the water and came to Jesus. But when he saw the wind, he was afraid, and beginning to sink he cried out, "Lord, save me." Jesus immediately reached out His hand and took hold of him, saying to him, "O you of little faith, why did you doubt?" (MATTHEW 14:28–31)

NEED A LITTLE MORE?

Peter stepped onto the raging waves with boldness and confidence when Jesus invited him to walk on the water. But the wind and the waves drew his eyes and attention away from Jesus, so Peter began to sink into the sea. Sometimes that happens when you face decisions. You feel like you're sinking quickly when you don't know what to do. The key to making decisions is to keep your eyes on Jesus. Read His Word, take time to pray, and listen to wise and godly people for guidance. Take time for this careful deliberation. Your Savior will reach out to you and pull you from the waves of confusion as you look to Him with trust and hope. Sometimes He will give you clear direction. At other times, He will let you know what not to do. In some circumstances, He will have you wait. But Jesus will never leave you on your own as you face decisions.

FAITH NOTES

Use the steps below as a pathway to decision-making:

Pray: Ask God for guidance. Then watch and listen for His direction.

Read God's Word: Pick a section of the Bible to read as you deliberate a decision. See how the Spirit guides you through the Word.

Consult wise and godly people: Ask trusted advisers to give input and help guide you.

Take time: If it's a quick decision, try to let one night pass before you decide. If you have more time to pray, read the Word and consult with people. Take up to forty days to see how God directs you.

8

LOOKING AHEAD: THE END AND THE BEGINNING

ONE-SENTENCE DEVOTION

Young man of God, you need to know that this world will come to an end and your life will come to an end, which is why Jesus provides miraculous hope and preparation for you: His resurrection for you and your resurrection to eternal life through faith in Him.

GOD'S WORD SPEAKS

Jesus said to [Martha], "I am the resurrection and the life. Whoever believes in Me, though he die, yet shall he live, and everyone who lives and believes in Me shall never die. Do you believe this?" (JOHN 11:25–26)

NEED A LITTLE MORE?

Do you believe that Jesus is the resurrection and the life? That's what Jesus asked Martha as she grieved over her brother's death. It's an important question for you. This world will come to an end, and your life will end. No one knows when you will die or when Jesus will return (see Mark 13:32), but you will see Jesus face to face at some point in the future (see Matthew 24:30–31). As a baptized child of God, forgiven and redeemed by Jesus, you don't need to be afraid of the end. Jesus loves you and will welcome you with open arms. He will embrace you with great joy. The most important part of your future is your eternal future. Eternity is a long time, and God wants to spend it with you. That's why He sent His Son to save you. Jesus prayed to His Father in heaven, "And this is eternal life, that they know You, the only true God, and Jesus Christ whom You have sent" (John 17:3). That is the gift you have been given. This is the new life from Jesus that leads to strength, peace, and joy. Who would want any other way? Believe and celebrate this blessing—and share it with everyone as you live by faith in your Friend and Savior, Jesus.

FAITH NOTES

If you haven't done it already, sign your name in the front of this book as a confession of the gift you've received—the good and beautiful gift of faith in Jesus.

FIFTY-TWO BIBLE VERSES FOR YOUR LIFE

When you need peace:
[Jesus said,] "Peace I leave with you; My peace I give to you. Not as the world gives do I give to you. Let not your hearts be troubled, neither let them be afraid." (JOHN 14:27)

When your heart is broken:
The LORD is near to the brokenhearted and saves the crushed in spirit. (PSALM 34:18)

When you feel alone:
Be strong and courageous. Do not be frightened, and do not be dismayed, for the LORD your God is with you wherever you go. (JOSHUA 1:9)

When you feel angry:
Be angry, and do not sin; ponder in your own hearts on your beds, and be silent. Offer right sacrifices, and put your trust in the LORD. (PSALM 4:4–5)

When talking is getting you in trouble:
Even a fool who keeps silent is considered wise; when he closes his lips, he is deemed intelligent. (PROVERBS 17:28)

When you need guidance about social media:
Let no corrupting talk come out of your mouths, but only such as is good for building up, as fits the occasion, that it may give grace to those who hear. (EPHESIANS 4:29)

When you feel like your sin is too big for God:
But God, being rich in mercy, because of the great love with which He loved us, even when we were dead in our trespasses, made us alive together with Christ—by grace you have been saved. (EPHESIANS 2:4–5)

When you need a new start:
If anyone is in Christ, he is a new creation. The old has passed away; behold, the new has come. (2 CORINTHIANS 5:17)

When you feel anxious:
Do not be anxious about anything, but in everything by prayer and supplication with thanksgiving let your requests be made known to God. And the peace of God, which surpasses all understanding, will guard your hearts and your minds in Christ Jesus. (Philippians 4:6–7)

When you are tempted by porn:
Finally, brothers, whatever is true, whatever is honorable, whatever is just, whatever is pure, whatever is lovely, whatever is commendable, if there is any excellence, if there is anything worthy of praise, think about these things. What you have learned and received

and heard and seen in me—practice these things, and the God of peace will be with you. (PHILIPPIANS 4:8–9)

When you are deciding what to put in your body:
Do you not know that your body is a temple of the Holy Spirit within you, whom you have from God? You are not your own, for you were bought with a price. So glorify God in your body. (1 CORINTHIANS 6:19–20)

When you wonder if anyone cares about you:
[Jesus said,] "For God so loved the world, that He gave His only Son, that whoever believes in Him should not perish but have eternal life. For God did not send His Son into the world to condemn the world, but in order that the world might be saved through Him." (JOHN 3:16–17)

When you feel overwhelmed:
[Jesus said,] "Come to Me, all who labor and are heavy laden, and I will give you rest." (MATTHEW 11:28)

When you need confidence:
I can do all things through Him who strengthens me. (PHILIPPIANS 4:13)

When you wonder if God is real:
The heavens declare the glory of God, and the sky above proclaims His handiwork. Day to day pours out speech, and night to night reveals knowledge. There is no speech, nor are there words, whose voice is not

heard. Their voice goes out through all the earth, and their words to the end of the world. (PSALM 19:1–4)

When you're sad:
Weeping may tarry for the night, but joy comes with the morning. (PSALM 30:5)

When you wonder if you have any talents:
Now there are varieties of gifts, but the same Spirit; and there are varieties of service, but the same Lord; and there are varieties of activities, but it is the same God who empowers them all in everyone. To each is given the manifestation of the Spirit for the common good. (1 CORINTHIANS 12:4–7)

When you wonder if God has a plan for your life:
For I know the plans I have for you, declares the LORD, plans for welfare and not for evil, to give you a future and a hope. (JEREMIAH 29:11)

When you wonder what to do with your troubles:
Cast your burden on the LORD, and He will sustain you; He will never permit the righteous to be moved. (PSALM 55:22)

When you wonder if God listens to you:
Call upon Me in the day of trouble; I will deliver you, and you shall glorify Me. (PSALM 50:15)

When you feel like your hurt is a waste:
As for you, you meant evil against me, but God meant it for good, to bring it about that many people should be kept alive, as they are today. (GENESIS 50:20)

When you feel like life's circumstances are too much for God:
For I am sure that neither death nor life, nor angels nor rulers, nor things present nor things to come, nor powers, nor height nor depth, nor anything else in all creation, will be able to separate us from the love of God in Christ Jesus our Lord. (ROMANS 8:38–39)

When bad news seems to have triumphed:
[Jesus said,] "In the world you will have tribulation. But take heart; I have overcome the world." (JOHN 16:33)

When you need forgiveness:
Come now, let us reason together, says the LORD: though your sins are like scarlet, they shall be as white as snow; though they are red like crimson, they shall become like wool. (ISAIAH 1:18)

When you experience sexual temptation:
For this is the will of God, your sanctification: that you abstain from sexual immorality. (1 THESSALONIANS 4:3)

When you want to live in step with the Holy Spirit:
But the fruit of the Spirit is love, joy, peace, patience, kindness, goodness, faithfulness, gentleness, self-control; against such things there is no law. And those

who belong to Christ Jesus have crucified the flesh with its passions and desires. If we live by the Spirit, let us also keep in step with the Spirit. (GALATIANS 5:22–25)

When you want to know the secret to a successful life:

Put on then, as God's chosen ones, holy and beloved, compassionate hearts, kindness, humility, meekness, and patience, bearing with one another and, if one has a complaint against another, forgiving each other; as the Lord has forgiven you, so you also must forgive. And above all these put on love, which binds everything together in perfect harmony. And let the peace of Christ rule in your hearts, to which indeed you were called in one body. And be thankful. Let the word of Christ dwell in you richly, teaching and admonishing one another in all wisdom, singing psalms and hymns and spiritual songs, with thankfulness in your hearts to God. And whatever you do, in word or deed, do everything in the name of the Lord Jesus, giving thanks to God the Father through Him. (COLOSSIANS 3:12–17)

When you need to know how to love someone:

Love is patient and kind; love does not envy or boast; it is not arrogant or rude. It does not insist on its own way; it is not irritable or resentful; it does not rejoice at wrongdoing, but rejoices with the truth. Love bears all things, believes all things, hopes all things, endures all things. Love never ends. (1 CORINTHIANS 13:4–8)

When you're wondering how to treat your parents:
Honor your father and your mother, that your days may be long in the land that the LORD your God is giving you. (EXODUS 20:12)

When you're tempted by drugs or alcohol:
Do not get drunk with wine, for that is debauchery, but be filled with the Spirit. (EPHESIANS 5:18)

When you need to know how to treat other people:
Be kind to one another, tenderhearted, forgiving one another, as God in Christ forgave you. (EPHESIANS 4:32)

When you need to know what Jesus has done for you:
But He was pierced for our transgressions; He was crushed for our iniquities; upon Him was the chastisement that brought us peace, and with His wounds we are healed. (ISAIAH 53:5)

When you need purpose:
I will make you as a light for the nations, that My salvation may reach to the end of the earth. (ISAIAH 49:6)

When you need to know what sin looks like:
[Jesus said,] "For from within, out of the heart of man, come evil thoughts, sexual immorality, theft, murder, adultery, coveting, wickedness, deceit, sensuality, envy, slander, pride, foolishness. All these evil things come from within, and they defile a person." (MARK 7:21–23)

When you need wisdom instead of foolishness:
The way of a fool is right in his own eyes, but a wise man listens to advice. (PROVERBS 12:15)

One who is wise is cautious and turns away from evil, but a fool is reckless and careless. (PROVERBS 14:16)

When you need to know how Baptism blesses you:
But when the goodness and loving kindness of God our Savior appeared, He saved us, not because of works done by us in righteousness, but according to His own mercy, by the washing of regeneration and renewal of the Holy Spirit, whom He poured out on us richly through Jesus Christ our Savior, so that being justified by His grace we might become heirs according to the hope of eternal life. (TITUS 3:4–7)

When you need to know how Holy Communion blesses you:
Jesus took bread, and after blessing it broke it and gave it to the disciples, and said, "Take, eat; this is My body." And He took a cup, and when He had given thanks He gave it to them, saying, "Drink of it, all of you, for this is My blood of the covenant, which is poured out for many for the forgiveness of sins." (MATTHEW 26:26–28)

When you need strength to endure:
[Jesus said,] "Be faithful unto death, and I will give you the crown of life." (REVELATION 2:10)

When you think you need to be perfect:
But God shows His love for us in that while we were still sinners, Christ died for us. (ROMANS 5:8)

When you don't know what to pray for:
Likewise the Spirit helps us in our weakness. For we do not know what to pray for as we ought, but the Spirit Himself intercedes for us with groanings too deep for words. (ROMANS 8:26)

When life is disappointing:
For I consider that the sufferings of this present time are not worth comparing with the glory that is to be revealed to us. (ROMANS 8:18)

When bad events seem to win:
And we know that for those who love God all things work together for good, for those who are called according to His purpose. (ROMANS 8:28)

When you wonder if other religions or philosophies are better than Christianity:
This Jesus is the stone that was rejected by you, the builders, which has become the cornerstone. And there is salvation in no one else, for there is no other name under heaven given among men by which we must be saved. (ACTS 4:11–12)

When you wonder if you're good enough:

For by grace you have been saved through faith. And this is not your own doing; it is the gift of God, not a result of works, so that no one may boast. For we are His workmanship, created in Christ Jesus for good works, which God prepared beforehand, that we should walk in them. (EPHESIANS 2:8–10)

When you need strength:

I have been crucified with Christ. It is no longer I who live, but Christ who lives in me. And the life I now live in the flesh I live by faith in the Son of God, who loved me and gave Himself for me. (GALATIANS 2:20)

When you need God's guidance:

Your word is a lamp to my feet and a light to my path. (PSALM 119:105)

When you need God's gifts to fight the spiritual battle:

Finally, be strong in the Lord and in the strength of His might. Put on the whole armor of God, that you may be able to stand against the schemes of the devil. For we do not wrestle against flesh and blood, but against the rulers, against the authorities, against the cosmic powers over this present darkness, against the spiritual forces of evil in the heavenly places. Therefore take up the whole armor of God, that you may be able to withstand in the evil day, and having done all, to stand firm. (EPHESIANS 6:10–13) **NOTE:** READ VERSES 14–18 TO SEE YOUR ARMOR.

When you feel weak:

But [Jesus] said to me, "My grace is sufficient for you, for My power is made perfect in weakness." Therefore I will boast all the more gladly of my weaknesses, so that the power of Christ may rest upon me. (2 CORINTHIANS 12:9)

When you think your hopes are impossible:

What no eye has seen, nor ear heard, nor the heart of man imagined, what God has prepared for those who love Him. (1 CORINTHIANS 2:9)

When you're ready to give up:

Even youths shall faint and be weary, and young men shall fall exhausted; but they who wait for the LORD shall renew their strength; they shall mount up with wings like eagles; they shall run and not be weary; they shall walk and not faint. (ISAIAH 40:30–31)

When you need eternal hope:

Jesus said to [Martha], "I am the resurrection and the life. Whoever believes in Me, though he die, yet shall he live, and everyone who lives and believes in Me shall never die. Do you believe this?" (JOHN 11:25–26)

INDEX OF SUBJECTS